Cambridge Elements

Elements in Eighteenth-Century Connections
edited by
Eve Tavor Bannet
University of Oklahoma
Markman Ellis
Queen Mary University of London

JACOBITISM AND CULTURAL MEMORY, 1688–1830

Leith Davis
Simon Fraser University

CAMBRIDGE
UNIVERSITY PRESS

Shaftesbury Road, Cambridge CB2 8EA, United Kingdom

One Liberty Plaza, 20th Floor, New York, NY 10006, USA

477 Williamstown Road, Port Melbourne, VIC 3207, Australia

314–321, 3rd Floor, Plot 3, Splendor Forum, Jasola District Centre,
New Delhi – 110025, India

103 Penang Road, #05–06/07, Visioncrest Commercial, Singapore 238467

Cambridge University Press is part of Cambridge University Press & Assessment,
a department of the University of Cambridge.

We share the University's mission to contribute to society through the pursuit of
education, learning and research at the highest international levels of excellence.

www.cambridge.org
Information on this title: www.cambridge.org/9781009548106

DOI: 10.1017/9781108986441

First published 2025

A catalogue record for this publication is available from the British Library

ISBN 978-1-009-54810-6 Hardback
ISBN 978-1-108-98661-8 Paperback
ISSN 2632-5578 (online)
ISSN 2632-556X (print)

Jacobitism and Cultural Memory, 1688–1830

Elements in Eighteenth-Century Connections

DOI: 10.1017/9781108986441
First published online: January 2025

Leith Davis
Simon Fraser University

Author for correspondence: Leith Davis, leith_davis@sfu.ca

Abstract: This Element has three objectives. First, it highlights the diversity of the nature of Jacobitism in the long eighteenth century by drawing attention to multi-media representations of Jacobitism and also to multi-lingual productions of the Jacobites themselves, including works in Irish Gaelic, Latin, Scots, Scots Gaelic and Welsh. Second, it puts the theoretical perspectives of cultural memory studies and book history in dialogue with each other to examine the process through which specific representations of the Jacobites came to dominate both academic and popular discourse. Finally, it contributes to literary studies by bringing the literature of the Jacobites and Jacobite Studies into the purview of more mainstream scholarship on eighteenth- and nineteenth-century literatures, providing a fuller perspective on the cultural landscape of that period and correcting a tendency to ignore or downplay the presence of Jacobitism.

This title is also available as Gold Open Access on Cambridge Core.

Keywords: Jacobites, cultural memory, eighteenth century, 1745, Scotland

ISBNs: 9781009548106 (HB), 9781108986618 (PB), 9781108986441 (OC)
ISSNs: 2632-5578 (online), 2632-556X (print)

Contents

1 Introduction: Jacobitism and Cultural Memory

On November 5, 1688, William of Orange, a Protestant Dutch nobleman, landed on the coast of Devon, England, and marched his sizeable army to London. After an aborted military conflict on Salisbury Plain, James II/VII, the ruling Catholic Stuart king, fled to France, and William and his wife Mary (James's daughter) subsequently became joint monarchs of England, Wales, Scotland and Ireland (see Figures 1 and 2). For a significant percentage of the population of the British Isles, however, who became known as the Jacobites (from the Latin for James, *Jacobus*), William and the Hanoverian monarchs who succeeded him were usurpers. Over the course of the next century, Jacobites in all four nations of the British Isles plotted continuously to restore the Stuart dynasty, drawing on international support when possible.[1] They took up arms against the government (or planned to) on a number of occasions. Moreover, in the course of both the 1715 rising (under James Edward Francis Stuart) and the 1745 rising (commanded by Charles Edward Stuart), the Jacobites experienced remarkable successes.[2] On April 16, 1746, however, the Jacobite cause was dealt a fatal blow at the Battle of Culloden. Although there continued to be Jacobite activity several decades after Culloden, including plans for another rising, a restoration of the Stuart dynasty became an impossibility after the death of Charles Edward Stuart in 1788.

Assessing the history of the Jacobites is difficult because it has been shaped over time by narratives that have settled into complex layers of affective cultural memories. From claims in 1688 that James II/VII's heir was illegitimate (the "warming pan" controversy) to assertions in 1745 regarding the slavish devotion of "barbaric" Highlanders to their clan leaders, disparaging narratives about the Jacobites were created and circulated during the era in which the Jacobites were active.[3] After the defeat of the Jacobites in 1746, these earlier narratives were amplified and extended by equally powerful narratives regarding the inevitability of the Jacobite defeat and romanticized versions of their history. Through such means, by the end of the eighteenth century, the actual threat to the British government that the Jacobites had posed earlier in the eighteenth century had been retrospectively minimized and reshaped, and, in the early nineteenth century, thanks to powerful narratives offered by literary and popular printed works, the Jacobites had become synonymous with noble, but ill-fated, struggle.[4] Both negative and sentimental cultural memories of the Jacobites

---

[1] I use the term "British Isles" throughout this Element, recognizing its limitations, particularly in regard to Ireland, but considering this the best option for referring to the four nations/three kingdoms in what is sometimes awkwardly referred to as the British archipelago.

[2] See Pittock, *Culloden* and Szechi, 1715.   [3] See Pittock, *Myth.*

[4] See Pittock, *Culloden* and *Poetry*; and Monod, *Jacobitism.*

Figure 1 Sir Peter Lely (1618–80) – James II/VII (1633–1701) when Duke of York. Public domain. Wikimedia Commons.

were also taken up by and entrenched within academic discourse in the nine-teenth and twentieth centuries.[5] Despite the emergence of careful new historical research on the Jacobites over the last several decades, traces of past perceptions continue to influence scholarly understanding of the Jacobites even in the

---

[5] See Pittock, *Culloden* and *Poetry*.

Figure 2 R. White. Engraving of William III and Mary II, 1703. Public domain.
Wikimedia Commons.

present day. At the same time, the overwhelming popularity of Diana
Gabaldon's *Outlander* books and the Starz television series based on the
books is testament to the way in which previous stereotypes developed about
the Jacobites continue to be perpetuated in popular culture.[6]

---

[6] See Davis, *Mediating*; and Davis and Mottiez, "Restory-ing."

1.1 Objectives

Jacobitism and Cultural Memory, 1688–1830 has three main objectives. First, it seeks to highlight the diversity of the nature of Jacobitism in the long eighteenth century. As Daniel Szechi notes, "Jacobitism in the British Isles was … a very complex phenomenon, involving national and confessional divisions in every one of the three kingdoms."[7] In discussing the discourse pertaining to the Jacobites, I consider both anti-Jacobite and pro-Jacobite productions throughout the British Isles. Important recent scholarship on Jacobitism has shed new light on the material culture of Jacobitism, investigating the way in which "Jacobite material culture substitutes for conventional and articulated text," creating its own coded language of symbol and often drawing on "fragmentary text … as a framework for shared memory."[8] Taking a different but complementary direction, I focus here solely on textual mediation, attending to works produced in a variety of media and genres, analyzing not just printed works but also works of manuscript culture and, where possible, traces of oral performance.[9] I seek to further expand the understanding of Jacobite culture by drawing attention not only to multimedia representations of the Jacobites but also to their own multilingual productions, including works in Irish Gaelic, Latin, Irish Gaelic, Latin, Scots and Scots Gaelic. To better understand the widespread nature of Jacobite affiliation, I have looked beyond what might be considered traditional literary works. In particular, I have taken account of the creation and circulation of popular printed works as well as the compilation and sharing of manuscript materials. The fact that so many of these ephemeral materials are still extant in archives today indicates the importance accorded them during their early circulation as well as the subsequent value placed upon them as worthy of preservation.[10]

The second objective of this Element is to put the theoretical perspectives of Cultural Memory Studies and Book History into dialogue with one another to examine the process through which specific representations concerning the Jacobites came to dominate over the course of nearly 150 years. I consider representations of the Jacobites within the context of a changing media environment in the eighteenth century, as I analyze how, within a growing market for print, narratives generated about the Jacobites became "spreadable" stories

---

[7] Szechi, 1715, p. 61. See also Pittock, *Poetry*; Lenman, *Jacobite Risings*; and McLynn, *Jacobites*.

[8] See Pittock, *Material Culture*, p. 3. See also Guthrie, *Material Culture*; and Coltman, *Art and Identity*.

[9] See Donaldson, *Jacobite Song*; and Pittock, "Scottish Song."

[10] On the continuity of manuscript culture in the eighteenth century, see Levy and Schellenberg, *How and Why*; and Schellenberg, *Literary Coteries*. On ephemeral print, see Russell, *Ephemeral Eighteenth Century*.

which were in turn recycled into other mediations to create enduring cultural memories.[11] Ann Rigney comments on the power of repetition in the creation of cultural memories: "It is because figures are relayed across media (image, texts), across discursive genres (literary, historiographical, judicial) and across practices (commemorations, judicial procedures, private reading) that they can end up becoming collective points of reference for individuals inhabiting different locations."[12] In the discussion that follows, I explore the mediations of figures and narratives that contributed to shaping the "collective point of reference" known as Jacobitism from 1688 to 1830, from the movement's earliest inception to the point at which there was a conscious perception that actual eye-witnesses to the last Jacobite rising had passed away. I consider both anti- and pro-Jacobite discourse, examining how, due to market considerations, aspects of both were frequently entangled within individual works of print. Such mediated complexities suggest how the nation of Britain was forged, in multiple senses of the word, out of knots consisting of both official memories and counter-memories.[13]

A third goal of this Element is to contribute to literary studies in general by bringing the literature of the Jacobites and Jacobite Studies into the purview of more mainstream scholarship on eighteenth- and nineteenth-century literatures, providing a fuller perspective on the cultural landscape of that period and correcting what has been a tendency to ignore and downplay the presence of Jacobitism. Pittock and other scholars have pointed out the prevalence of Jacobite affiliation in the eighteenth century: "Jacobites and associated nationalist views and beliefs were sometimes the sympathies of many, and always those of a significant minority."[14] Yet the Jacobite cause has been largely marginalized within the literary historical record. As Joseph Hone asserts, while "few topics have provoked quite so much ire among historians of the period" as Jacobite historiography, "most literary scholars ignore the wider phenomenon except where it concerns major authors such as Samuel Johnson."[15] The most recent (2024) edition of the *Norton Anthology of English Literature*, for example, minimizes the political uncertainty caused by

---

[11] The editors of *Spreadable Media: Creating Meaning and Value in a Networked Culture* employ the term "spreadable" to refer to "the technical resources that make it easier to circulate some kinds of content than others, the economic structures that support or restrict circulation, the attributes of a media text that might appeal to a community's motivation for sharing material, and the social networks that link people" (Jenkins et al., *Spreadable Media*, p. 4).

[12] Rigney, "Dynamics," p. 350.   [13] See Davis, *Acts of Union*, pp. 13–14.

[14] Pittock, *Poetry and Jacobite Politics*, p. 3.

[15] Hone, *Alexander Pope*, p. 3. For a general comparison, a search of the term "Jacobite" on the MLA International Bibliography between 2014 and the present yields 40 peer-reviewed articles on topics spread out between 1688 and 1850; a search of the term "French Revolution," however, yields 392 results.

Jacobites in the first half-century after 1688. Even while acknowledging that "a good many writers … privately sympathized with Jacobitism," the editors inadvertently reinforce the Whig perspective on the eighteenth century, asserting that "in retrospect, the accession of William and Mary in 1688 – the Glorious, or Bloodless, Revolution – came to be seen as the beginning of a stabilized, unified Great Britain" and listing the "innovations" that "made this stability possible."[16] In 2004, Daniel Szechi remarked that "the prevailing orthodoxy on the long eighteenth century is going to remain flawed and misleading until it can encompass apparent anachronisms like the Jacobite movement."[17] Szechi's comment is still relevant twenty years later. Accordingly, this Element will address the marginalization of Jacobitism in literary history as well as drawing attention to the continued existence of Jacobite counter-memories.

In the remainder of this Introduction, I provide an overview of the theoretical perspectives of Cultural Memory Studies and Book History that I draw together in this Element, and I outline the media changes taking place in the eighteenth century that enabled the initial suppression and later marginalization of the Jacobite cause. I also suggest the ways in which Cultural Memory Studies can offer a way of understanding the entanglement of memories and counter-memories that existed within this complex media landscape.

1.2 Cultural Memory Studies and Mediation

Cultural Memory Studies is an area of research that has expanded exponentially since the 1990s to become what Meike Bal identifies as a "travelling concept," one that moves "between disciplines, between historical periods, and between geographically dispersed academic communities."[18] It has been enormously influential in literary studies, particularly in relation to the twentieth-century and contemporary periods. The origins of Cultural Memory Studies can be traced back to the work of the French sociologist Maurice Halbwachs (1877–1945), who, in *Les cadres sociaux de la mémoire* (published originally in 1925), coined the term "mémoire collective," or "collective memory." According to Halbwachs, an individual's memories are in fact "a part of an aspect of group memory" because they are fundamentally "connected with the thoughts that come to us from the social milieu."[19]

---

[16] Greenblatt, Noggle and Smith, *Norton Anthology*, p. 6.
This material is also repeated in the condensed version of the *Norton Anthology*, Vol. 1, p. 1032. https://wwnorton.com/books/9781324062929. The editors' employment of the terms "glorious" and "bloodless" to describe the 1688 Revolution and their buttressing of the sense of "stability" that resulted from this event are called into question by the perspectives included in this Element. Online version. C-6/
[17] Szechi, 1715, p. 7.   [18] Bal, *Travelling*, p. 24.   [19] Halbwachs, 53.

Halbwachs' death in a Nazi concentration camp prevented him from developing his ideas further. Nevertheless, a new interest in collective memory arose in the 1980s and 1990s, in part amid general concern that the rapid changes in society would erode a sense of history and that with the passing of eye-witnesses to the traumatic events of the Holocaust, that event in particular would fade from memory.[20] The two focal geographical locations for the next phase in the development of Cultural Memory Studies were European countries: Germany and France. In Germany, Halbwachs' ideas were taken up by Jan Assmann and Aleida Assmann. In *Cultural Memory and Early Civilization* (2011), Jan Assmann, an Egyptologist by training, attempts to determine the nature of that which he describes as the "connective structure" in all cultures that "links yesterday with today by giving form and presence to influential experiences and memories, incorporating images and tales from another time into the background of the onward moving present, and bringing with it hope and continuity."[21] Assmann modified Halbwachs' theories in order to distinguish between "communicative memory," which, he suggests, has a "limited temporal horizon" confined to the living memory of the group experiencing the memory, and "cultural memory," or the form of memory that becomes fixed when "living communication crystalliz[es] in the forms of objectivized culture – whether in texts, images, rites, buildings, monuments, cities or even landscapes."[22] Concurrently, in her work, Aleida Assmann considers memory from the perspectives of more recent forms of literature and cultural anthropology, exploring how cultural memories are created, stored and altered over time. In *Cultural Memory and Western Civilization: Functions, Media, Archives* (2011), Aleida Assmann draws attention to the distinction between "stored" memory, which, she suggests, consists of "an amorphous mass of elements," and "functional" memory which "emerges from a process of choosing, connecting and constituting meaning."[23] Both the Assmanns, then, have been explicitly focused on the media through which cultural memories were created, stored and circulated.

At the same time during which the Assmanns were honing their theories, the French historian Pierre Nora was developing his notion of *lieux de mémoire*, or sites of memory, influenced by the work of Frances Yates in *The Art of Memory* (1966). According to Nora, people in the contemporary era are no longer organically connected to their communities through shared living memories (*milieux de mémoire*). Instead, he argues, specific sites of memory (*lieux de mémoire*) take on the role of preserving a sense of connection to the past.

---

[20]　See Davis, "Memory Studies."

[21]　J. Assmann, *Cultural Memory and Early Civilization*, p. 2.

[22]　J. Assmann and Czaplicka, "Collective Memory," p. 128.

[23]　A. Assmann, *Cultural Memory*, p. 137.

A *lieu de mémoire*, Nora asserts, can be "any significant entity, whether material or non-material in nature, which by dint of human will or the work of time has become a symbolic element of the memorial heritage of any community."[24] Although he indicates that sites of cultural memory can be either "material or non-material," Nora, unlike the Assmanns, does not explicitly analyze the media through which the cultural memories are passed down. Moreover, in contrast to the comparative approach that the Assmanns adopted, Nora concentrates on national sites of memory in France. The popularity of Nora's work, particularly within North American academic contexts, however, has served to expand geographical and disciplinary reach of Cultural Memory Studies exponentially.

In this Element, I draw on the work of critics who have been influenced by but who also critique and extend the work of the Assmanns and Nora to consider further the implications of "the evolution of media technology" on cultural memory.[25] I follow the lead of Ann Rigney and Astrid Erll, for example, who argue that it is only possible to understand the "dynamics" of cultural memory if we examine "not just the social factors at work," but also "the 'medial frameworks' of remembering and the specifically medial processes through which memories come into the public arena and *become* collective."[26] In *Memory in Culture,* Erll expands on the work of Aleida Assmann as she offers a detailed explanation of how the "functional potential" of any memory media is connected not just to their "material components" but also to the "social frameworks" in which they are used "by individuals, social groups, and societies" and that sometimes involve "forms of institutionalization."[27] Once "functionalized" within these social contexts, Erll asserts, "media of memory" are either stored for later re-activation or circulated; alternatively, they might become "cues" (similar to Nora's *lieux de mémoire*) which trigger cultural remembrance. Erll also notes, however, that "whenever media are studied as parts of memory culture, they must be removed from a generalizing, ahistorical view, and seen in relationship to very specific cultural processes."[28] Bearing in mind Erll's observation regarding the importance of historicizing media, the following section of this Element draws attention to specific ways in which cultural memory of the Jacobites emerged from within the complexities of the changing media landscape of the British Isles in the long eighteenth century as it shifted to an era of print saturation.[29] The subsequent section carries this investigation forward into the late eighteenth and early nineteenth centuries, examining how the stored memories, both pro- and anti-Jacobite, converge and are re-activated within the contemporary political and social contexts.

---

[24] Nora and Kritzman, *Realms*, p. xvii.   [25] J. Assmann, *Cultural Memory*, p. 2.
[26] Erll and Rigney, "Mediation," p. 2.   [27] Erll, *Memory in Culture*, 124.
[28] Erll, *Memory in Culture*, 125.   [29] Multigraph Collective, *Interacting*.

1.3 A Book History Approach to the Cultural Memory of Jacobitism

The period during which the Jacobites were actively working to reinstate the Stuart monarchy, the early to mid eighteenth century, coincided with a significant change in the mediascape in the British Isles as print came to assume a more dominant role in the media ecologies of all four nations. Clifford Siskin and William Warner suggest that print was coming to take "center stage" within the context of an "already existing media ecology of voice, sound, image, and manuscript writing."[30] The print marketplace in England expanded after 1695 when parliament failed to renew the Licensing Act that had been created under the regime of Charles II. The lapse of this act ended pre-circulation censorship and allowed for an increase in the number of presses in England. Also contributing to the growth in the print marketplace were the increase in literacy rates, the creation of better infrastructure such as roads and regular postal routes and, in 1710, the passing of the copyright law.[31] As we will see in subsequent sections, these changes were accompanied by a marked increase in the publication of printed books, pamphlets and singles, as well as the expansion of newspaper publication and the development of a robust periodical press.[32] But, although the lapse of the Licensing Act meant that printed works did not need official approval prior to printing, government agents could nevertheless prosecute what was considered treasonous material. Records of Jacobite culture were therefore more likely to be communicated using the more exclusive media of manuscript and oral culture rather than print. Figure 3, a drinking song titled "Come let uss goe drink boyes," and Figure 4, a "[A Paraphrase Upon] Psalm 137," provide examples of Jacobite-affiliated items that circulated in manuscript form. The wear and tear as seen in the creases on both items suggests that these were carried around on the owner's person and perhaps even passed between individuals.

The restrictions on the "functionalization" of Jacobite memory media meant that Jacobite media of cultural memory did not have the same potential for storage and circulation as anti-Jacobite media of cultural memory. They were not as "spreadable," to use the term of Jenkins et al. Erll and Rigney note that it is the "inter-medial reiteration of [a] story across different platforms in the public arena (print, image, internet, commemorative rituals)" that enables cultural memory to "take root in the community."[33] In an eighteenth-century context, not surprisingly, it was the anti-Jacobite mediations that prevailed. Nevertheless, as I also demonstrate in this Element, traces of Jacobite counter-memories can still be discerned,

---

[30] Siskin and Warner, "This is Enlightenment."   [31] McDowell, "Media and Mediation."

[32] See King, *Writing to the World* and *After Print.*

[33] Erll and Rigney, "Introduction," *Mediation*, pp. 2–3.

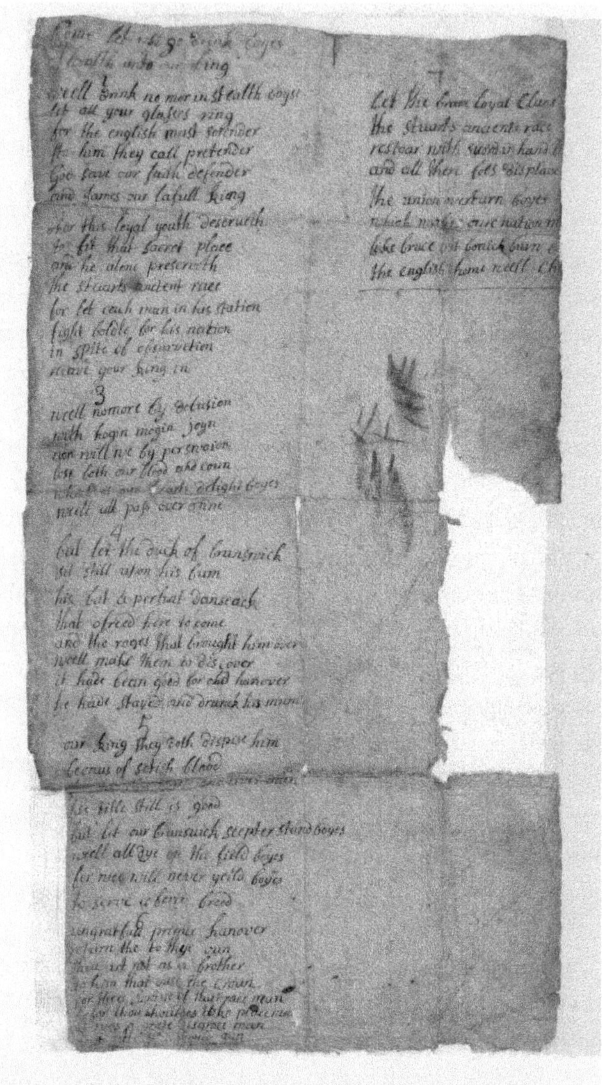

Figure 3 "Come let uss goe drink boyes." Jacobite Papers MS 1696. f. 90v. Courtesy of National Library of Scotland.

sometimes even within the anti-Jacobite printed archive, as eighteenth-century printers drew on a variety of materials in order to boost sales of their titles. Once fixed in print, these Jacobite counter-memories, however attenuated or coded, also enjoyed a wider circulation and, in turn, were reproduced in subsequent works. In examining such entangled anti-Jacobite and pro-Jacobite perspectives, I draw in particular on the work of Michael Rosenberg who proposes the

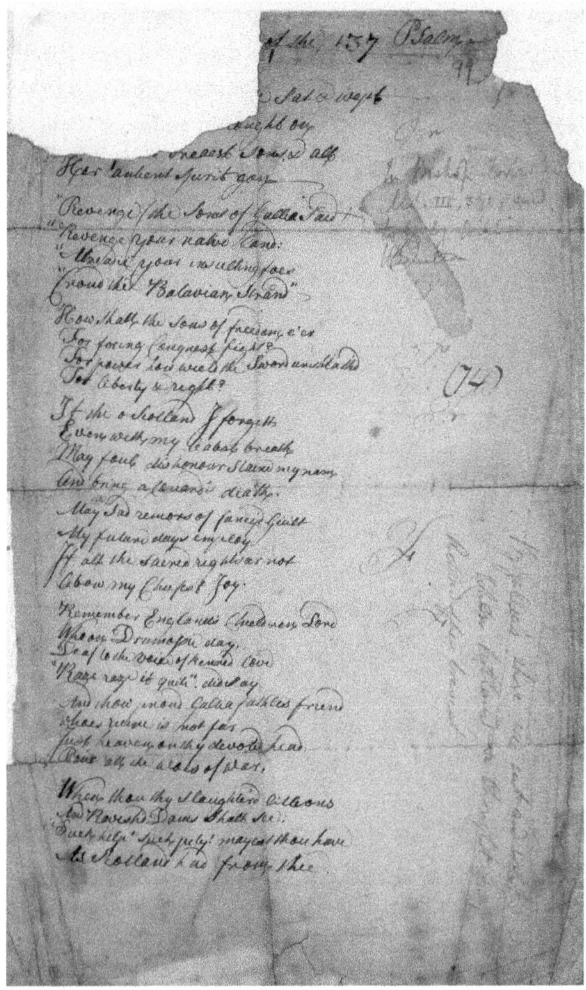

Figure 4 "[A Paraphrase Upon] Psalm 137." Jacobite Papers MS 1696. f. 99r.
Courtesy of National Library of Scotland.

metaphor of *noeuds de mémoire* (knots of memory) as a replacement for Nora's more static concept of *lieux de mémoire* (sites of memory).[34] In Rothberg's formulation, *noeuds de mémoire* constitute "rhizomatic networks of temporality and cultural reference that exceed attempts at territorialisation . . . and identarian reduction."[35] The model of *noeuds de mémoire* reflects the complex relationship between dominant and counter-memories perceptible in this crucial time of media change. As I suggest in my readings throughout this book, texts of knotted

---

[34] Rothberg, "Introduction," p. 7.　　[35] Rothberg, "Introduction," p. 7.

memory can lean variously toward or away from "identitarian reduction"; in other words, they can resonate to a greater or lesser extent with one specific ideological perspective. Nevertheless, even rigidly Jacobite or anti-Jacobite texts often also register traces that brush against their articulated political grain, making themselves available for re-shaping and/or re-activation in other mediations.[36]

Before going forward, it is important to acknowledge several important factors impacting my analysis of the construction of the knots of cultural memory of Jacobitism in this changing mediascape. To begin with, I draw heavily on popular works as well as what might be considered more standard works of literature. Many of the materials that I examine here (especially those that were produced hastily during the time of print expansion) were designed for immediate popular consumption, not for literary posterity. Adam Fox's comments regarding printed material circulating in Scotland hold true for the rest of Britain and Ireland at the time, as he notes that the "press-work that most of the population came into regular contact with" consisted of "small items of practical use or popular appeal that were sold on the streets, hawked around the country, or posted up in public" rather than what might today be considered literary works.[37] Such items were usually "made of the poorest quality paper, left unbound and sold on the streets."[38] The broadside ballad "A Race at Sherriff-Muir" (Figure 5) serves as an example of such ephemeral popular works.

Written from the narrative perspective of one who "sa" the battle between the Jacobites and the government forces on "13 November 1715," "A Race at Sherriff-Muir" was printed on cheap paper with a woodcut illustration to give it additional popular appeal. Designed for consumption by supporters of both the government and the Jacobite sides, the broadside represents a knot of memory as it celebrates and satirizes soldiers from both camps, encouraging engagement by providing new lyrics to a familiar tune, "the HORSEMANS SPORT." The narrator of the broadside draws attention to the ephemeral purpose of the work as he compares his own feeble efforts at "Rime" with the work of Alexander Robertson of Struan ("Strowan the witty/A poet that pleases us a[ll] Man"). Nevertheless, this Element suggests that such works as "A Race at Sherriff-Muir" are as important literary artifacts as more recognized literary works; they were in fact consumed and enjoyed by a larger and more diverse number of people.

At the same time as analyzing popular and literary printed works in this Element, I also call attention to the difference between the media landscapes of

---

[36] This investigation takes a different route from Pittock's theorization of Jacobite cultural memory which reads the ambiguity only in Jacobite materials (see *Material Culture*, pp. 1–21). I suggest the ideological entanglement in texts by writers occupying multiple political positions.

[37] Fox, "The Press," p. 2.   [38] Fox, "The Press," p. 6.

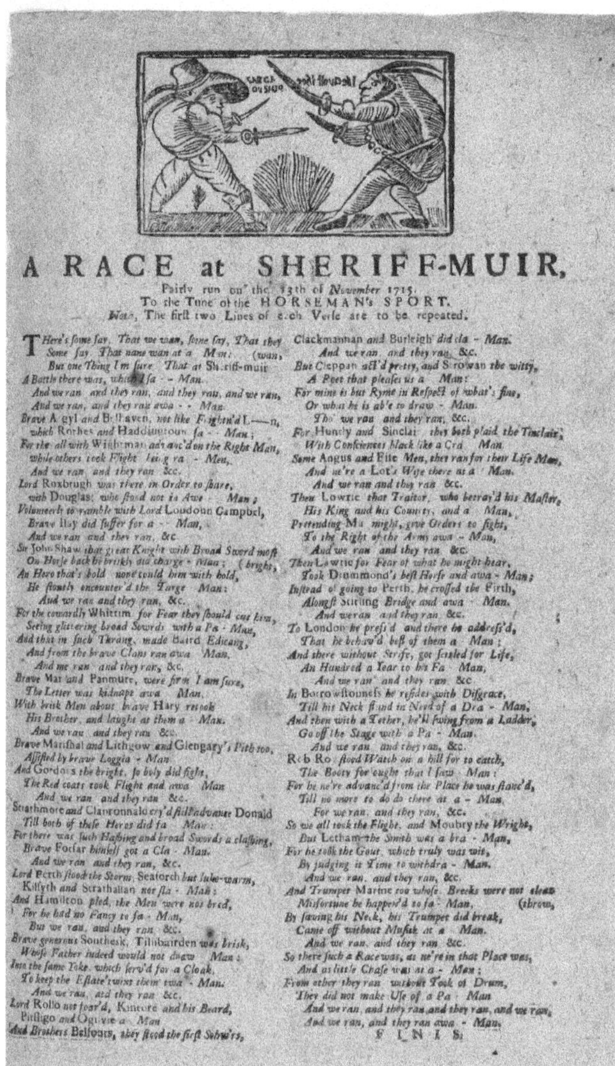

Figure 5 "A Race at Sherriff-Muir." Jacobite Relics. MS. 2960 f. 46. Courtesy of National Library of Scotland.

England, Scotland, Ireland and Wales during the long eighteenth century. In Lowland Scotland, as Karin Bowie notes, the expansion of print culture at the beginning of the eighteenth century approximated that which occurred in England during the lapse of the Licensing Act.[39] A corresponding shift occurred in the English-language print marketplace in Ireland. James Raven observes

---

[39] Bowie, *Public Opinion.*

that, whereas Dublin was the main location of printing activity in the seventeenth century, over the course of the eighteenth century, printing in Ireland expanded "to include almost all Irish towns and market centres."[40] Within the Scots Gaelic and Irish Gaelic traditions, however, the media landscapes were significantly different. As Domhnall Uilleam Stiùbhart notes, "Scots Gaelic-language 'literature' remained predominantly oral in nature, fluid and hybrid" during the seventeenth to the mid eighteenth centuries, even though it was also intersecting with and responding to "written classical or semi-classical poetry."[41] A similar media fluidity pertained in the case of Irish Gaelic literature, where there was also a blending of "Gaelic language manuscript culture with classically inflected poetic utterance."[42] As Niall Ó Ciosáin notes in *Print and the Celtic Language: Publishing and Reading in Irish, Welsh, Gaelic and Breton, 1700–1900,* "Printing in Irish was extremely sparse in the early eighteenth century."[43] The fortunes of Irish Gaelic and Scottish Gaelic literatures took divergent pathways after 1745 and the defeat of the Jacobites, however, as there was a concerted effort to render the Scots Gaelic language into print after Culloden. The situation in Wales, which had been politically incorporated into England in the sixteenth century, was different still. The majority of the population of Wales was Welsh-speaking. Printing of Welsh-language works was much more extensive than Scots and Irish Gaelic works, occurring first in London, where there was a sizeable Welsh population, and then in Shrewsbury. As Evans and Fulton point out, "by the second quarter of the eighteenth century, printing in Wales itself was properly established with locally produced books competing for the first time with Welsh books from the London trade."[44] Space prevents me from further discussion of the literary and linguistic particulars of each of the Celtic-language nations, however the main point here is that that the entities known as England, Wales, Scotland and Ireland before 1707 and as Great Britain and Ireland after that date included complex mediascapes in which oral, manuscript and print cultures had different relative values. Oral and manuscript traditions were particularly prominent and highly valued in the geopolitical peripheries of the British Isles. It is therefore crucial to keep in mind what John Kerrigan calls an "archipelagic" perspective regarding the changing mediascape as we examine the multilingual and multimedia contexts of Jacobitism across the four nations and three kingdoms.[45]

---

[40] Raven, "Non-metropolitan Printing"; See also Brownlees.

[41] Stiùbhart, "Adaptation,"; See also Thomson, "Gaelic poetry."

[42] Brown, "Jacobite Baroque."

[43] Ó Ciosáin, *Print,* p. 56. See also Constantine and Leask, "Introduction."

[44] Evans and Fulton, "Introduction," p. 7.   [45] Kerrigan, *Archipelagic English.*

Finally, it is also critical to bear in mind that even in areas in which print saturation was more prominent, the media environment was still complex. Recent scholarship has focused on the continuing role of manuscript culture within Britain despite the increasing shift to print, and oral forms of communication were of course still ubiquitous.[46] Printed content was created in and then circulated through different media. A broadside ballad might be composed either orally or in manuscript, then printed, advertised by a ballad-singer through oral performance and sold to a consumer or displayed in a coffee house for further circulation and/or performance; it might also be remediated into a more durable form in a songster or cheap poetry collection. A sermon could be handwritten, then delivered orally as well as being printed; it could then be discussed and excerpted in commonplace books by members of the congregation. In other words, what we now think of as printed texts were both created and shared inter-medially.

1.4 Explanation of Sections

Eneken Laanes and Hanna Meretoja assert that "Just like individual narratives exist in narrative environments shaped by the dynamics of master and counter-narratives, cultural memorial forms exist in memorial environments in which some memorial forms are dominant and others marginalised."[47] *Jacobitism and Cultural Memory, 1688–1830* demonstrates how anti-Jacobite master narratives dominated in the eighteenth century and influenced the cultural memory of the Jacobites in the following eras. At the same time, however, it asserts that by closely examining the representations of Jacobitism within the changing media ecology of the eighteenth and early nineteenth centuries, we can shed light on the way in which Jacobite counter-memories persisted even within the dominant official British cultural memory. Moreover, this Element contends that drawing attention to the marginalized Jacobite voices that appear within an official cultural memory strategically designed to minimize them also allows us to consider connections to cultural remembering and forgetting in other contexts beyond Jacobitism. Going forward, Section 2 outlines how the rapid development of print culture impacted the creation of the cultural memory of the Jacobites in the long eighteenth century. Section 3 then examines the reshaping of the cultural memory of the Jacobites in the early nineteenth century. I conclude by considering the refashioning of Jacobitism at that point when it was passing from communicative into cultural memory as the last eye-witnesses were passing on.

---

[46] See Levy and Schellenberg, *How and Why*; and Schellenberg, *Literary Coteries*.
[47] Laanes and Meretoja, "Editorial," p. 6.

2 Shaping Jacobitism, 1688–1746

One of the most pervasive misapprehensions concerning the cultural memory of the Jacobites is the idea that Jacobite activity in the long eighteenth century was confined to three outbreaks of armed conflict: the initial resistance to the 1688 arrival of William of Orange (which is typically seen as confined to Ireland) and the armed risings of 1715 and 1745 (historically referred to officially as "rebellions"). Although, for purposes of organization, I have divided this section into three parts corresponding to these three major episodes of military resistance, it is important to bear in mind that there was constant Jacobite activity taking place during the time between the arrival of William of Orange and the death of Charles Edward Stuart in 1788, as the Jacobites were engaged in continual efforts to overthrow the sitting monarchs. These efforts included diplomatic discussions and negotiations with European players as well as plans for military interventions. In addition, there continued to be a steady stream of correspondence, a constant circulation of individuals and groups and a robust flow of goods between Jacobites in locations in Britain and Europe as well as across the Atlantic throughout the long eighteenth century. Daniel Szechi suggests that by focusing on the range of Jacobite activities and events, we can better understand the inherent political instability of the British Isles during this time period, as he notes that Jacobite activity included all of the following: "a brief insurrection in the Highlands in 1719, and abortive attempts by France to invade the British Isles in conjunction with planned Jacobite uprisings in 1692, 1696, 1708, 1744, 1745 and 1759, and by Spain in 1719," plus "plots and conspiracies" that were discovered in "1689–90, 1704, 1716–17, 1720–2, 1725–7, 1730–2 and 1750–2" and "serious conspiracies that fizzled out before drastic intervention was called for in 1709–10, 1713–14 and 1758–9."[48] As Szechi suggests, "On average there was a serious Jacobite-related 'event' in the British Isles every one to two years between 1689 and 1722, and every three to four years between 1740 and 1760."

Jacobite followers in each of the three kingdoms of the British Isles had different national, economic and confessional motivations. Nevertheless, they were in agreement about the same central objective: the re-establishment of the Stuart dynasty. A crucial aspect of advocating and preparing for the restoration of the Stuarts therefore involved keeping the cause alive through cultural means, a task that was not easy given the legal proscription against Jacobitism as well as the sheer amount of anti-Jacobite discourse in circulation. Murray Pittock notes that "the laws on treason and

---

[48] Szechi, "Jacobite Movement," 83.

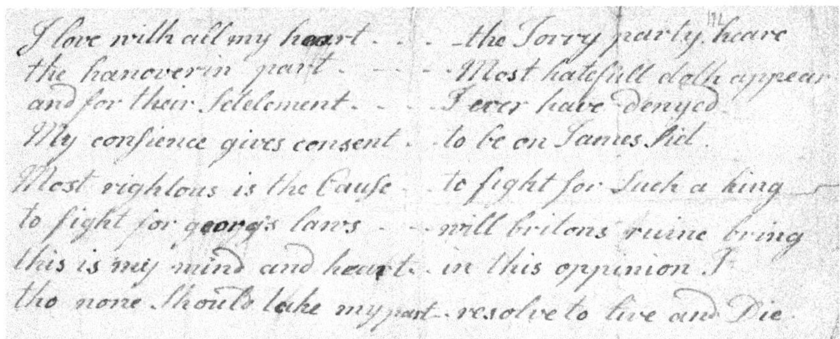

Figure 6 Cryptic Jacobite poem: "I love with all my heart." La.II.358.f.172. Courtesy of The University of Edinburgh, Heritage Collections.

sedition" were a substantial check on "Jacobite discourse, language, symbol, association, communication, and display."[49] As Pittock observes, the laws "could be very severe in their effects, not infrequently bearing the risk of a capital charge." Adherents of the Jacobite cause therefore frequently resorted to coded communications, particularly after 1716, to avoid detection and prosecution. Figure 6, for example, demonstrates a cryptic Jacobite poem. Read vertically as two stanzas, the poem asserts its devotion to "the hanoverian part" and "georg[e']s laws." Read horizontally across the page, however, the words promote "the Torry party" and assert the speaker's intention to fight for King James.

In the sections that follow, I discuss a wide variety of mediations, cryptic and otherwise, that were used to shape the memories of the Jacobites from the 1688 Revolution to the aftermath of the Battle of Culloden – cultural memories created by those who sought to minimize and eradicate the Jacobite threat as well as memories put into circulation by the Jacobites themselves. I include published literary works, but I also analyze more ephemeral works such as broadsides, popular pamphlets and newspapers and manuscript materials. The general focus of this section is to provide a fuller understanding of the diversity of the discourse on the Jacobite cause between 1688 and 1746. While I examine the trajectory of how pro-Hanoverian perspectives came to dominate in the construction of official cultural memory of Jacobitism within the changing eighteenth-century mediascape, I also consider the way in which the counter-memories shaped by the Jacobites themselves sometimes appeared within pro-government interventions, forming the complex knots of memory referred to in the Introduction.

---

[49] Pittock, *Material Culture*, p. 4.

2.1 Remembering the 1688 Revolution

The regime change that later became referenced by anti-Jacobites as the "Glorious" or "Bloodless" Revolution of 1688 was precipitated by concerns in England regarding the religious affiliation and governing strategies of the Catholic King James II/VII, who had succeeded his brother Charles II in 1685. Upon his ascension, James set out to promote Catholic interests, adopting strategic policies that included religious tolerance and "intervention in local government," thus alienating vast numbers of his subjects.[50] The subsequent birth of a son, James Francis Edward Stuart, to James and his wife, Mary of Modena, brought the issue to a head, as it became clear that the next monarch to inherit the thrones of England, Ireland and Scotland would be James's Catholic son, rather than one of his Protestant daughters, Mary or Anne. Accordingly, seven prominent Protestant noblemen contacted William pledging support for a potential military intervention. For his part, William was interested in strengthening his connection with England in order to help him with his wars with the Catholic powers in Europe.

The regime change that took place in 1688–89 was not only the culmination of a successful military campaign; it also represented a unique media event in British history as it constituted the deliberate shaping of a *lieu de mémoire* for the nation through a campaign involving popular print.[51] In *The Social History of the Media: From Gutenberg to the Internet*, Asa Briggs and Peter Burke comment on the creation of the cultural memory of 1688: "The fact that we still refer to the events of 1688 as the 'Glorious Revolution' testifies to the power of an image which was consciously fabricated at that time."[52] That fabrication began even before William's landing, as printed works, pamphlets and engravings that disparaged James circulated in England. One rumor called into question the legitimacy of James's son by suggesting that the baby had been smuggled into the Queen's bedroom in a warming pan.[53]

In addition, shortly before the launch of the Dutch invasion, William and his advisors, including the Dutch Gaspar Fagel and the Scottish historian and Episcopalian minister and later bishop Gilbert Burnet, produced a pamphlet which framed the invasion as an intervention that was necessary to protect the Protestant religion and to rescue the English nation from the clutches of James and his evil advisors (see Figure 7). *The Declaration of His Highness William Henry . . . of the Reasons Inducing him, to appear in Arms in the Kingdome of*

---

[50] Raffe, *Scotland in Revolution*, p. 1. See also Harris, *Revolution*; and Pincus, *1688*, as well as Clark, *English Society*.

[51] See Davis, *Mediating Cultural Memory*, ch. 1.   [52] Briggs and Burke, *A Social History*, p. 78.

[53] Some of these works had in fact printed in the Dutch republic and distributed in England.

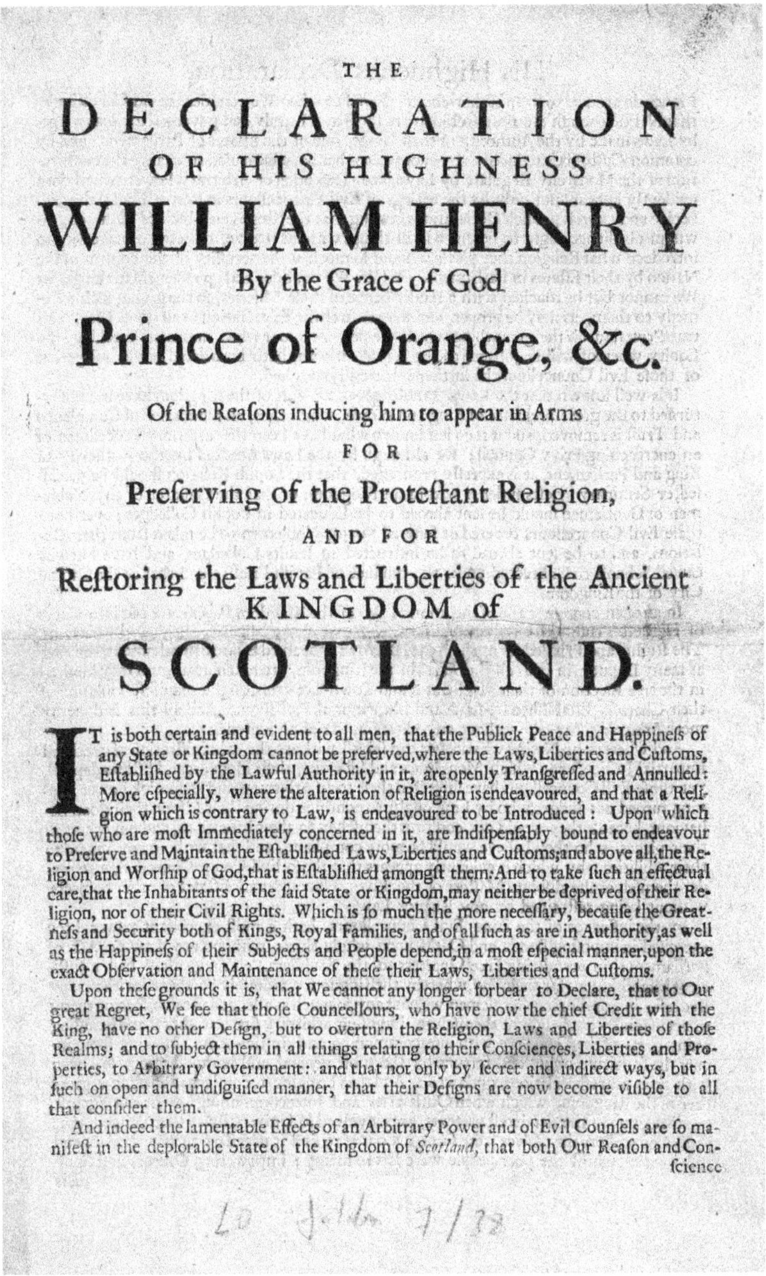

THE
DECLARATION
OF HIS HIGHNESS
WILLIAM HENRY
By the Grace of God
Prince of Orange, &c.

Of the Reasons inducing him to appear in Arms

FOR

Preserving of the Proteſtant Religion,

AND FOR

Reſtoring the Laws and Liberties of the Ancient
KINGDOM of
SCOTLAND.

IT is both certain and evident to all men, that the Publick Peace and Happineſs of any State or Kingdom cannot be preſerved, where the Laws, Liberties and Cuſtoms, Eſtabliſhed by the Lawful Authority in it, are openly Tranſgreſſed and Annulled: More eſpecially, where the alteration of Religion is endeavoured, and that a Religion which is contrary to Law, is endeavoured to be Introduced : Upon which thoſe who are moſt Immediately concerned in it, are Indiſpenſably bound to endeavour to Preſerve and Maintain the Eſtabliſhed Laws, Liberties and Cuſtoms; and above all, the Religion and Worſhip of God, that is Eſtabliſhed amongſt them. And to take ſuch an effectual care, that the Inhabitants of the ſaid State or Kingdom, may neither be deprived of their Religion, nor of their Civil Rights. Which is ſo much the more neceſſary, becauſe the Greatneſs and Security both of Kings, Royal Families, and of all ſuch as are in Authority, as well as the Happineſs of their Subjects and People depend, in a moſt eſpecial manner, upon the exact Obſervation and Maintenance of theſe their Laws, Liberties and Cuſtoms.

Upon theſe grounds it is, that We cannot any longer forbear to Declare, that to Our great Regret, We ſee that thoſe Councellours, who have now the chief Credit with the King, have no other Deſign, but to overturn the Religion, Laws and Liberties of thoſe Realms; and to ſubject them in all things relating to their Conſciences, Liberties and Properties, to Arbitrary Government: and that not only by ſecret and indirect ways, but in ſuch on open and undiſguiſed manner, that their Deſigns are now become viſible to all that conſider them.

And indeed the lamentable Effects of an Arbitrary Power and of Evil Counſels are ſo maniſeſt in the deplorable State of the Kingdom of *Scotland*, that both Our Reaſon and Conſcience

Figure 7 *The Declaration of His Highness William Henry . . . of the Reasons Inducing him, to appear in Arms in the Kingdome of England.* Courtesy of the National Library of Ireland.

England was pre-printed in Holland and released in numerous locations in England and Scotland after the landing. Ann Rigney suggests the way that successful sites of cultural memory build upon previous sites of memory. Demonstrating Rigney's principle, the *Declaration* foregrounds the Magna Carta and the "ancient laws."

The impact of the *Declaration* on the cultural memory of William's "appearance" in the British Isles cannot be underestimated. Although there had been published declarations associated with other would-be claimants to the throne (including those by the Duke of Montrose and the Duke of Argyll who took up arms against James at the beginning of his reign in 1685), this was the first time in Britain that there had been such a focus on managing the public perception of a military venture while it was being undertaken. Lois Schwoerer observes that, by 1688, "English people were well accustomed to the public airing in print of political and religious commentary and ideas that were sharply critical of the government," and that this "background of experience with the print media" was "an important part of the context within which the Revolution unfolded."[54] It was certainly important enough for James himself to issue a proclamation on November 2, 1688, making it illegal to "Publish, Disperse, Repeat or Hand about" or "Read, Receive, Conceal or Keep" the *Declaration* of the Prince of Orange.[55]

The importance of the *Declaration* as a printed document was also affirmed by its remediation in other contexts. Notably, the *Declaration* was read out at significant locations as William made his way to London. *An Account Of the Proceedings and Transactions that have Happened in The Kingdom Of England, Since The Arrival Of The Dutch Fleet, and the Landing of The Prince of Orange's Army* indicates that the recitation of the *Declaration* was part of William's official ceremony at Exeter Cathedral: "He entering that City in much Splendor, and with the loud Huzza's and Shouts of the People, the Bells Ringing, and the Bonefires [sic] at night flaming in every Street . . . And here it was that His Highness's Declaration, relating His Intentions for the preservation of the Protestant Religion, and Redressing the Grievances of the Nation, by removing Evil Counsellors, &c. was published, more especially publickly Read."[56] Other locations in which it was read publicly include Bath (November 20, 1688) and Oxford (December 6, 1688). The importance of the *Declaration* is also suggested by the fact that it is referred to in a number of popular ballads at the time. Even when they did not refer to it directly, popular ballads also echoed the

---

[54] Schwoerer, "Liberty of the Press," p. 220.   [55] James II, *By the King.*
[56] *An Account of the Proceedings*, pp. 2–3.

language and position of the *Declaration*. The ballad "A New Touch of the Times. OR, The Nations [sic] Consent, For a Free Parliament," for example, suggests that "Loyalty" to the Prince of Orange is a patriotic duty for all "*English true-hearted Boys*":[57]

> Rejoyce, rejoyce all ye brave English Hearts,
> Since Popery from our Nation must depart,
> For the Prince will have a Free Parliament,
> And they bravely will settle our Government:
> Then let every honest true-hearted man,
> Do their endeavour as near as they can,
> For to uphold the Prince in the way of Right,
> Against the Pope and their Jesuits spight.[58]

Along with the promotion of the nation and the preservation of the Protestant religion, the ballad highlights the desire for economic improvement as well: "I hope that *brave Trading hereafter we shall see,*/And plenty of work for the poor there will be." Another broadside published for the occasion, entitled "A Full Description of these Times; Or The Prince of ORANGE's March from EXETER to LONDON," similarly lauds "The Brave Prince of Orange" who has "been our best friend/And routed all Popery out of the Land."[59]

Both broadsides call for and look forward to a "free Parliament." After James fled from Whitehall on December 23, 1688 (after being unceremoniously returned following an earlier attempt to escape) and William was given the responsibility for governing, such a parliament was indeed called, although, because it was hastily convened before a new election could be held, it was comprised of members elected during the reign of Charles II.[60] The resulting Convention Parliament, so-called, assembled in England in January 1689, was tasked with settling the question of the rule of the nation. After much debate, the Convention determined that James had abdicated the throne. Before offering William and Mary the Crown of England, however, the Convention also required them to agree to the terms of a Bill of Rights that would limit monarchical power. As Lois Schwoerer notes, this bill was in fact based on the points that had been made in William's *Declaration*.[61]

During the extensive media campaign that took place during this time and after, both anti- and pro-Williamite works drew on the memory of the nation's past to accuse each other of promoting despotism and slavery and leading the nation to economic ruin. Critics of 1688 emphasized the unnaturalness of

---

[57] *A New Touch of the Times.*   [58] *A New Touch of the Times.*

[59] *A Full Description of These Times.*   [60] Burnet, *A Compleat History.*

[61] See Schwoerer, *Declaration.*

William's actions (as he was both nephew and son-in-law of James), the political irregularity of events (the summoning of the Convention Parliament did not follow proper precedent) and the immorality of deposing a king who had been anointed by God. Pro-Williamite works emphasized the providential aspect of the Revolution and the restoration of "Rights and Liberties" in order to focus attention away from the extraordinary circumstances through which the Stuart dynasty had been unseated.[62] Those supporting the Williamite cause sought to confirm the new regime by condemning the illegitimacy of James's son, representing James as a tyrannical despot and praising William's benevolence in saving the Protestant faith. In *The History of the Desertion*, for example, Edmund Bohun reprinted the official documents that were published during the events of 1688, providing his own commentary to guide the reader toward viewing the 1688 Revolution as a positive event. Bohun reinforces the importance of William's words rather than his military exploits, noting that "wherever the Prince's *Declaration* was read, it conquered all that saw or heard it."[63] As Kelsey Jackson Williams points out, William even had one of the special services of the Book of Common Prayer altered as he authorized the addition of the celebration of "the Happy Arrival of His present Majesty" to the "Thanksgiving" service on November 5 for the salvation of James I/VI from the Gunpowder plot.[64] Although ultimately the Williamite side came to dominate in the printed discourse of the day, as we will see, Jacobites would continue to draw on the same language of illegitimacy and despotism in making their claims against the established government.

The circumstances of the Revolution unfolded differently in Scotland. As Alasdair Raffe suggests, the main impetus for the regime change in Scotland was not unhappiness with James's policies but the reality of William's victory in England: "the breakdown of its government and the construction of a successor regime were enabled by the invasion of, and successful seizure of power in, England."[65] Although the Convention of Estates that met in Scotland in March offered the throne to William and Mary on April 11, 1689 (which they accepted on May 11, 1689), the Scottish Convention had come to a different rationale for this decision than had the Convention Parliament in England, determining instead that James had forfeited his right to rule as a result of his policies. They also set out to establish a Revolution Settlement, "a series of political and religious reforms," that were not in fact confirmed until 1690.[66] The decision to offer the throne to William and Mary was contested in Scotland, however, as, in March 1689, John Graham of Claverhouse, 1st Viscount Dundee led a military

---

[62] Burnet, *Compleat History*, 9.   [63] Bohun, *History*, 71.
[64] Williams, "Archibald Pitcairne's Liturgical Year," p. 11.   [65] Raffe, p. 4.   [66] Raffe, p. 132.

rising in support of James that became known as the Highland War. The Scottish Jacobites were victorious at the Battle of Killiecrankie on July 27, 1689, although Dundee himself was killed during the battle. The Highland War subsequently shifted to a series of guerrilla attacks until a settlement was signed in June 1691, with those who had taken up arms against William being required to relinquish their weapons and swear an oath of allegiance before January 1, 1692. On February 13, 1692, thirty members of the MacDonald clan were murdered at Glencoe by members of the Campbell clan as punishment for not obeying the order to disarm in time. This event subsequently became one of the most searing cultural memories in Scots Gaelic culture.

The so-called "Bloodless" Revolution of 1688 was also far from bloodless across the Irish Sea.[67] Because the population of Ireland was roughly 80 percent Catholic, James II/VII's program of religious tolerance and the promotion of Catholic interests had been welcomed in that nation. Apart from areas in Ulster that were largely Presbyterian, Ireland remained loyal to James after the Williamite victory in England. James himself landed in Ireland in March 1689 to try to regain his kingdoms with of the support of French troops and funds. The subsequent conflict in Ireland, known as the War of the Two Kings (*Cogadh an Dá Rí* in Irish Gaelic), did not go well at first for William's forces. The relief of the three-month-long siege of Derry in July 1689, however, was seen as a change in fortune for the Williamite cause, and that siege subsequently became the focus of celebration for many pro-Williamite published works which would contribute to the narrative of the cultural memory of the 1688 Revolution. Works like *A True Account of the Siege and Famous Defence made at London-Derry* by George Walker, who had been a governor of Derry during the siege, encouraged the branding of the 1688 Revolution as an act of providence by connecting it with the sufferings and eventual salvation of Protestants during an earlier Irish *lieu de mémoire*, the 1641 Rebellion.[68] Such works came with fold out maps to provide images of the conflict for readers outside Ireland. Figure 8, for example, combines a topographical sketch of the region around Derry with chronologically compressed visual representations of important military moments in the lifting of the siege.

The War of the Two Kings finally came to a conclusion in October 1691 with the signing of Treaty of Limerick (*Conradh Luimnigh* in Gaelic). Again, pro-Williamite works attempted to create a narrative favorable to the new government. In relaying "our short (but Glorious) History," the author of *A Diary of the Siege & Surrender of Lymerick: With the Articles at Large: Both Civil and*

---

[67] Burton, in his *Compleat History*, provides a tally of over 10,000 soldiers Irish killed during the conflict in Ireland.

[68] The engraving of Walker also appeared in the title page of *A True Account*.

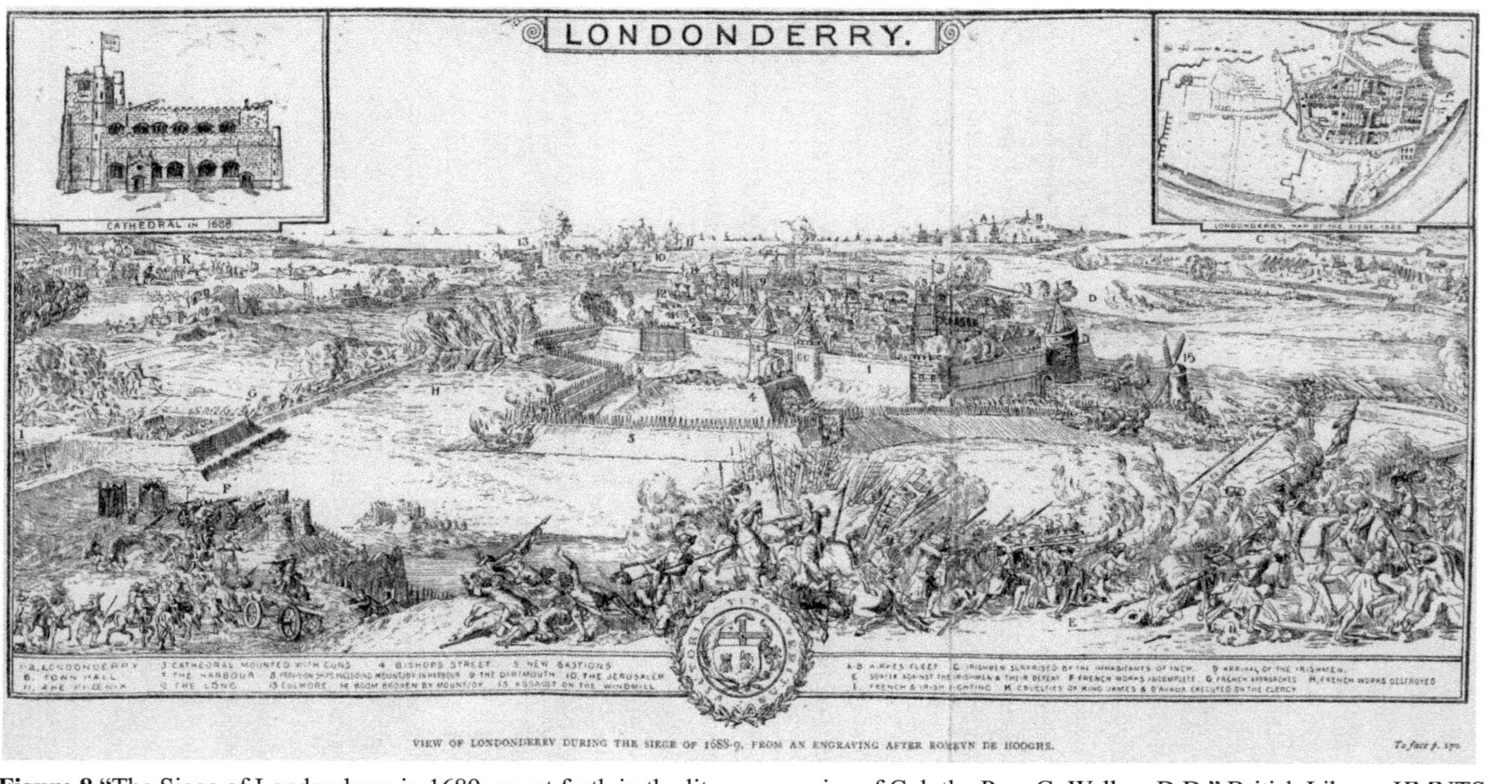

Figure 8 "The Siege of Londonderry in 1689, as set forth in the literary remains of Col. the Rev. G. Walker, D.D." British Library HMNTS 9509.c.7. Public domain.

Military, represents the final victory of William's troops as the culmination of "a continued chain of Providences."[69] Ignoring the fact that many of the troops who fought in Ireland were Dutch, the author draws attention to the way in which these providential events are also part of a wider history of "British" cultural memory, as he suggests that the progress of "English Armes in Ireland" has as much "Signaliz'd the True British Valour, as any of the Antiquer Monuments of our Remoter Recorded Predecessors." *A Diary of the Siege & Surrender* also reinforces the representation of William as a merciful monarch concerned with the liberty of his subjects. The concessions made toward the Irish are such as to "plainly" tell "the World" that "the whole business of his Arms was to Reclaim, not Vanquish: He infringes no Liberty, even where he makes Subjection."[70]

The Treaty of Limerick promised many things. It assured Roman Catholics in Ireland "such Privileges in the Exercise of their Religion, as are consistent with the Laws of Ireland; or as they did enjoy in the Reign of King *Charles* II."[71] It offered those "Officers and Souldiers" in James's commission who submitted to William and Mary's "Obedience" the same "Rights, Titles and Interests, Privileges and Immunities" that they enjoyed in the reign of Charles II. It also allowed "all Persons" to "have free Liberty to go to any Countrey beyond the Seas (*England* and *Scotland* excepted) where they think fit, with their Families, Houshold-Stuff, Plate and Jewels" and provided for "all General Officers, Colonels and generally all other Officers" to be transported beyond the seas. In fact, roughly nineteen thousand military personnel left Ireland. As a result of this mass exodus, Irish participation in subsequent Jacobite risings was centered for the most part in France and other European locations, although support for the Jacobite cause remained strong amongst the Gaelic-speaking peoples in Ireland.[72]

2.2 Forging the Dominant Cultural Memory of the 1688 Revolution

Ann Rigney writes that "narrativization helps make particular events memorable by figuring the past in a structured way that engages the sympathies of the reader or viewer."[73] The narrativization of the Revolution as a "Glorious" act of God was reinforced by Williamite supporters as they attempted to forge a lasting positive cultural memory of recent events. Anticipating a critique of William after his death by the king's "Enemies," Abel Boyer in his *The History of King William the Third. In III Parts* (1702–03) asserts defensively that William "never acted out of any private Interest; but solely, in an Uprightness and Sincerity of Conscience, to do good to all Mankind in general, and to his

---

[69] *A Diary of the Siege & Surrender*, n.p.
[70] *A Diary of the Siege & Surrender*, The Publisher to the Reader," n.p.
[71] *A Diary of the Siege Surrender*, p. 25.   [72] See Ó Ciardha, *Ireland and the Jacobite Cause.*
[73] Rigney, "Dynamics," p. 347.

Subjects in particular; to preserve the Liberties of Christendom, and maintain the Protestant Religion in all Parts of Europe."[74] Another contemporary work, *Princely Excellency: or, Regal Glory. Being an Exact Account of the most Glorious Heroick, and Matchless Actions, of That Most Serene and Potent Prince, William the Third*, praises William as "the (Pater Patriae) the Father of our Country" and declares "To him, under God, we owe all the Blessings we now enjoy; our *Liberties, Religion*, and *Estates*, nay, our very Lives."[75] In the same vein, *The Triumphs of William III. King of England, Scotland, France and Ireland* compares William to the "Demi-gods" of "Ancient Times" but notes that whereas the heroes of "Antiquity" performed their deeds only "in favour of their Country, or rather to get themselves a Name," William's sole concern was to advance Glory of the King of Kings."[76]

These works also emphasized the ideological connection between William and his successor, Queen Anne, the second Protestant daughter of James II/VII, in order to further reinforce the narrative of the 1688 Revolution as a providential act. Boyer, for example, suggests that "as Queen ANNE was eminently instrumental in the late Revolution, so her Government stands upon the same Basis with that of King *William*."[77] The "Epistle Dedicatory" to Queen Anne in *Princely Excellency* concludes that, under Anne's "benign Government," "we hope to see our Rights, Liberties, and Religion continued."[78] Printed broadsides also circulated describing popular events that were also designed to reinforce the providential narrative of the 1688 Revolution and its continuity into Anne's reign, as can be seen in the broadside describing "the Burning of the Devil the Pope and the Pretender" that took place at Charing Cross on Anne's birthday on February 9, 1714"[79] (see Figure 9).

As Anne was childless, she and her government and supporters sought to ensure the continuity of a Protestant monarch in her kingdoms. In 1701, William had passed the Act of Settlement stipulating that any future monarch on the thrones of England and Ireland needed to be of the Protestant faith. But Scotland maintained its own parliament which theoretically could choose a different monarch. To avoid any possibility of Scotland's parliament settling on a Stuart heir, therefore, Anne appointed commissioners to negotiate a political union between England and Scotland. After a complicated period of negotiation

---

[74] Boyer, *The History of King William the Third.*

[75] J.A. "To the Reader," *Princely Excellency.*

[76] Beek, "Epistle Dedicatory" in *The Triumphs of William III.*

[77] Boyer, "Dedication," *History of King William,* Part II, n.p.

[78] *Princely Excellency,* "Epistle Dedicatory," n.p.

[79] NLS MS.2960. f. 28 "An Exact Account of the great Concourse of People of all Degres that were Actors and Spec[t]ators, at the procession, At the Burning of the Devil the Pope and the Pretender, at Charing-cross, near White hall, on Her Majesties Birth Day."

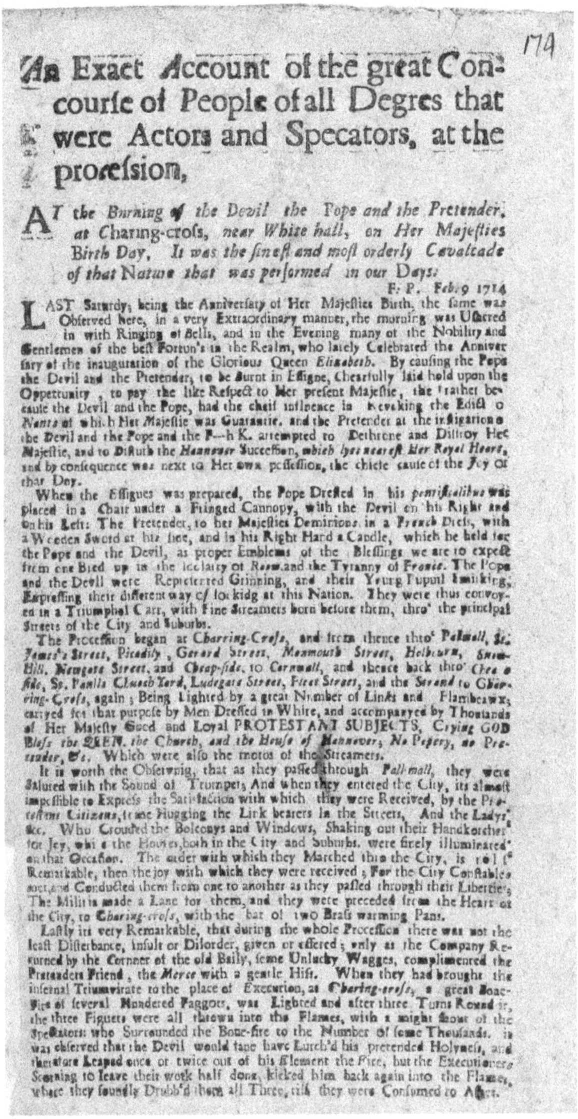

An Exact Account of the great Con-
courſe of People of all Degres that
were Actors and Specators, at the
proceſsion,

AT the Burning of the Devil the Pope and the Pretender,
at Charing-croſs, near White hall, on Her Majeſties
Birth Day, It was the fineſt and moſt orderly Cavalcade
of that Nature that was performed in our Days.

F. P. Feb. 9 1714

LAST Saturdy, being the Anniverſary of Her Majeſties Birth, the ſame was Obſerved here, in a very Extraordinary manner, the morning was Uſhered in with Ringing of Bells, and in the Evening many of the Nobility and Gentlemen of the beſt Fortun's in the Realm, who lately Celebrated the Anniverſary of the inauguration of the Glorious Queen Eliſabeth. By cauſing the Pope the Devil and the Pretender, to be Burnt in Effigne, Chearfully laid hold upon the Oppertunity, to pay the like Reſpect to Her preſent Majeſtie, the rather becauſe the Devil and the Pope, had the cheif influence in Revoking the Edict of Nants of which Her Majeſtie was Guarantie, and the Pretender at the inſtigation of the Devil and the Pope and the F—h K. attempted to Dethrone and Diſtroy Her Majeſtie, and to Diſturb the Hannover Succeſſion, which lyes neareſt Her Royal Heart, and by conſequence was next to Her own poſſeſſion, the chiefe cauſe of the Joy of that Day.

When the Effigues was prepared, the Pope Dreſſed in his pontificalibus was placed in a Chair under a Fringed Cannopy, with the Devil on his Right, and on his Left: The Pretender, to her Majeſties Demiſions, in a French Dreſs, with a Wooden Sword at his ſide, and in his Right Hand a Candle, which he held for the Pope and the Devil, as proper Emblems of the Bleſſings we are to expect from one Bred up in the Idolatry of Rome, and the Tyranny of France. The Pope and the Devill were Repreſented Grinning, and their Young Pupil Smirking, Expreſſing their different way of looking at this Nation. They were thus convoyed in a Triumphal Carr, with Fine Streamers born before them, thro' the principal Streets of the City and Suburbs.

The Proceſſion began at Charring-Croſs, and from thence thro' Palmall, St. James's Street, Picadily, Gerard Street, Monmouth Street, Holbourn, Snow-Hill, Newgate Street, and Cheap-ſide, to Cornwall, and thence back thro' Chea o ſide, St. Paulls Church Yard, Ludgate Street, Fleet Street, and the Strand to Charing-Croſs, again; Being Lighted by a great Number of Links and Flambeaux, carryed for that purpoſe by Men Dreſſed in White, and accompanyed by Thouſands of Her Majeſty Good and Loyal PROTESTANT SUBJECTS, Crying GOD Bleſs the QUEEN, the Church, and the Houſe of Hannover, No Popery, no Pretender, &c. Which were alſo the motos of the Streamers.

It is worth the Obſerving, that as they paſſed through Pall-mall, they were Saluted with the Sound of Trumpets And when they entered the City, its almoſt impoſſible to Expreſs the Satisfaction with which they were Received, by the Proteſtant Citizens, ſome Hugging the Link bearers in the Streets, And the Ladys, &c. Who Crouded the Bolconys and Windows, Shaking out their Handkorcheſ for Joy, whi e the Houſes, both in the City and Suburbs, were firely illuminated on that Occaſion. The order with which they Marched thro the City, is roll'd Remarkable, then the joy with which they were received; For the City Conſtables met and Conducted them from one to another as they paſſed through their Liberties, The Militia made a Lane for them, and they were preceded from the Heart of the City, to Charing-croſs, with the bar of two Braſs warming Pans.

Laſtly it is very Remarkable, that during the whole Proceſſion there was not the leaſt Diſterbance, inſult or Diſorder, given or offered; only as the Company Returned by the Corner of the old Baily, ſome Unlucky Wagges, complimented the Pretenders Friend, the Merce with a gentle Hiſs. When they had brought the infernal Triumvirate to the place of Execution, at Charing-croſs, a great Bone-Fire of ſeveral Hundered Faggots, was Lighted and after three Turns Round it, the three Figures were all thrown into the Flames, with a mighty ſhout of the Spectators who Surrounded the Bone-fire to the Number of ſome Thouſands. it was obſerved that the Devil would fane have Lurch'd his pretended Holyneſs, and therefore Leaped once or twice out of his Element the Fire, but the Executioners Scorning to leave their work half done, kicked him back again into the Flames, where they ſoundly Drubb'd them all Three, till they were Conſumed to Aſhes.

Figure 9 "An Exact Account of the Great Concourse of People of all Degres [sic] that were Actors and Spectators, at the procession." Jacobite Relics. MS.2960 f.28. Courtesy of National Library of Scotland.

of the Articles of Union (see Figure 10), the Acts of Union were eventually passed by both parliaments, and, in May 1707, the new united nation of Great Britain came into existence.[80]

---

[80] See Davis, *Acts of Union*; Jackson, *Two Unions*; and Whatley, *Scots and the Union*.

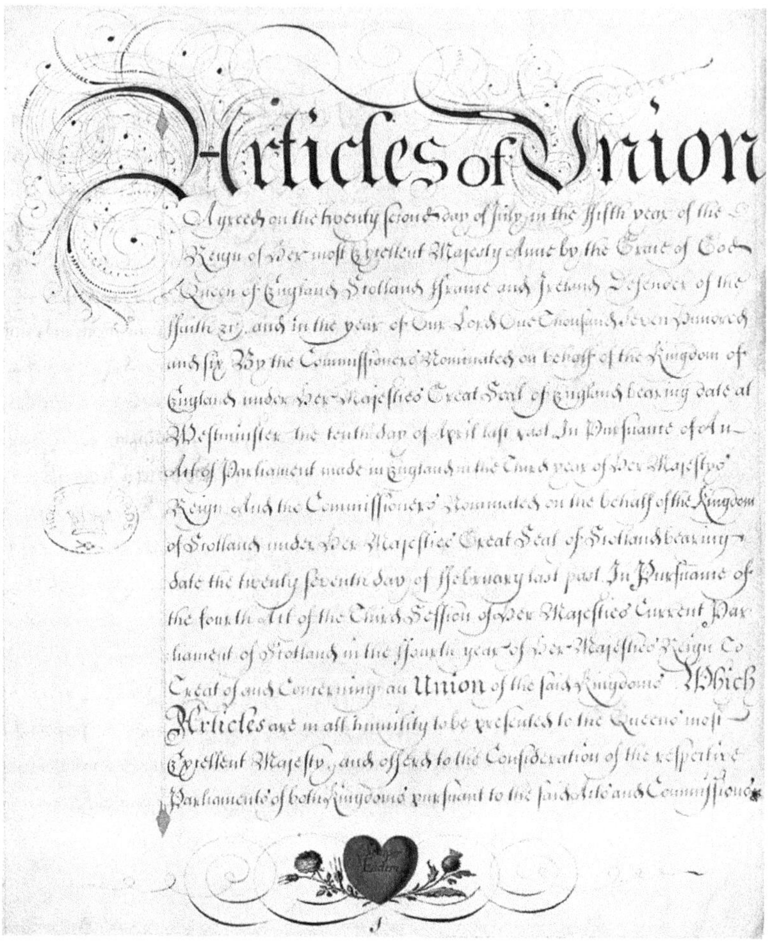

Figure 10 Articles of Union, 1706. Parliament of England, Public domain. Wikimedia Commons. Public Domain.

Popular print works celebrating the Union built on and amplified the earlier narratives of a providential plan guiding the British nation. In his *History of the Union*, for example, Daniel Defoe, who had worked in Scotland to promote the Union, suggested that the joining of the two nations represented a "Threed [*sic*] of History" that was a predestined occurrence,[81] asserting that the "various Turns the Island of *Britain* has had in the Compass of a few past Years" led inevitably "to this great Event."[82] *The Union-Proverb* (1708), also attributed to Defoe, similarly celebrates the "*happy consequences*" of an "ENTIRE UNION" that will lead to British nation being settled as "*One People*" under a "*right*

---

[81] Defoe, *History,* p. 45.   [82] Defoe, *History*, p. 1.

Foundation" of a Protestant monarchy.[83] Such a *"lasting Union"* that removes all *"invidious* Distinctions," he indicates, will "make the *Britains* a rich and flourishing People" in the future.[84] Moreover, *The Union-Proverb* also draws on contemporary concerns about Jacobites to justify the recent political negotiations, claiming that the Union will help protect both nations against "the circumventing Attempts of an aspiring MONARCH, who is still using his utmost *Efforts* to *inslave* both Nations."[85] The work suggests that the union of Scotland and England will help repel the Jacobites both internal and external to the nation, and, correspondingly, that the threat of Jacobitism will further encourage the unification of Great Britain: "Nothing again can make us so *warlike* and *formidable* to our *Enemies*, either in our own *Bosoms*, or at St. GERMAINS, as this glorious UNION upon a right and a sure Bottom."[86] Even as the pamphlet celebrates "so fair, so faithful, and so happy an Union," however, it also comments that "'tis to be hop'd, that the unfortunate Business of DARIEN will be *forgotten*; that the cruel Affair of GLENCOW will be forgiven; and that all exasperating *Reflexions*, or ignominious *Provocations*, will be wholly *forborn* on *both sides* for the future."[87] *The Union-Proverb* self-consciously recognizes the multiple acts of amnesia and selective remembering that constitute the construction of dominant memory narratives.

2.3 Jacobite Counter-narratives

While writers like Boyer and Defoe attempted with more or less success to weave the "Threed" of Britain's history into a cohesive narrative of providence and progress, pro-Jacobite writers and other cultural figures in the late seventeenth and early years of the eighteenth century forged very different narratives surrounding the 1688 Revolution and its aftermath. English writers such as Jane Barker, John Dryden, Anne Finch and Katherine Phillips continued to espouse the Stuart cause after 1688 both in manuscript and in print.[88] Barker, for example, dedicated her manuscript volume, "A Collection of Poems Refering [sic] to the times," "To his Royal Highness the Prince of Wales." Diminishing herself as an "insect scribler"[89] and "a person whose fingers are made to wield the needle and distaf [sic]" and who therefore "must not presume to write the character of so great a Prince," she nevertheless takes on the role of celebrating the young Stuart heir, praying for his "glories" to increase until "their splendor disperse all vapors of Rebellion and faction, and extinguish those blasing meteors, whose influence has caus'd so much ruin

---

[83] Defoe, *Union-Proverb*, p. 3 and p. 9.   [84] Defoe, *Union-Proverb*, p. 9.
[85] Defoe, *Union-Proverb*, p. 11.   [86] Defoe, *Union-Proverb*, pp. 11–12.
[87] Defoe, *Union-Proverb*, p. 13.   [88] See Pittock, *Poetry*, and Monod, *Jacobitism*.
[89] Barker, "To His Royal Highness the Prince of Wales," "A Collection of Poems," f. 5 recto.

and mischiefs to mankind."[90] Barker employs allegorical language in her collection, indicating that she has made her main character Fidelia "speak the common Dialect of Catholicks, and her friend the Church of England."[91] But Fidelia's story is also a secret history of Barker herself who followed James II/VII to the court at St. Germain. English Jacobite writers also turned to other kinds of coded narratives in order to allusively lament contemporary political circumstances and to promote the cause of the Stuart dynasty. As Nicole Horejsi confirms, the story of Aeneas, the founder of Rome, was particularly resonant of "the plight of the Stuart monarchy."[92] Dryden's 1697 translation of the *Aeneid*, for example, represents the adventures of a hero who, "forced by Fate/And haughty *Juno's* unrelenting Hate," is "Expell'd and exil'd" from his country, but who, after "Long Labours" and "doubtful War," sees his "banish'd Gods restor'd to Rites Divine,/And setl'd sure Succession in his Line."[93] The fulfilment of the restoration myth is also suggested by Alexander Pope in *Windsor-Forest* (1713) as he celebrates the return of the Stuart monarchy with the accession of Anne: "Peace and Plenty tell, a STUART reigns."[94] The Jacobite sympathies of Pope and other early eighteenth-century English Tory writers such as Jonathan Swift, Ann Finch and others have been the subjects of considerable critical debate, much of which focuses on the ambiguity of their work. As Joseph Hone asserts, for example, "Many of Pope's friends, mentors, patrons, and collaborators [in the first phase of his career] were active Jacobite conspirators,"[95] and Pope subsequently "maintained contact with the Jacobite underground" throughout his career, "even after having announced his retirement from political activity."[96]

Jacobites in the Scottish Lowlands similarly adopted coded or classical tropes to articulate their political sympathies, also responding to recent events, including the Acts of Union, by focusing on the Scottish nation's history and culture. The Jacobite printers Andrew Symson and Robert Fairbairn produced a version of *Virgil's Æneis* translated into Scots by Gavin Douglas (1710), while works such as James Watson's three-volume *Choice Collection of Comic and Serious Scots Poems both Ancient and Modern* (1706–1711) and George Mackenzie's *Lives and Characters of the most Eminent Writers of the Scots Nation* (1708) implicitly critiqued Defoe's idea of eliminating "*invidious* Distinctions" by

---

[90] Barker, "To His Royal Highness the Prince of Wales," "A Collection of Poems," f. 6 recto.

[91] Barker, "To the Reader," "A Collection of Poems," 7 verso.

[92] Horejsi, *Novel Cleopatras*, p. 25. While writers such as Dryden reinforced this resonance, Horejsi suggests that Barker revises the triumphalist focus of the *Aeneid*, "expand[ing] notions of heroism and refut[ing] the limitations of traditional epic and history" (27). See also Eicke, "Jane Barker's Jacobite Writings" and Keegan and Hoxmeier.

[93] Dryden, *Works of Virgil*, p. 201.   [94] Pope, *Windsor-Forest*, p. 2.

[95] Hone, *Alexander Pope*, p. 2.   [96] Hone, *Alexander Pope*, p. 8.

emphasizing Scottish cultural and political uniqueness. Other works from the popular press were less concerned about masking their affiliations.

Scots Gaelic and Irish Gaelic poets also voiced their opposition to the Williamite regime change. But whereas English and Lowland Scottish Jacobite-leaning writers expressed their views in print, often employing "innuendo and ambiguity" to conceal their political affiliations, most of existing corpus of seventeenth-century Scots Gaelic poetry, including the work of Sìleas na Ceapaich (Cicely Macdonald of Keppoch) (c. 1660–1729), Iain Dubh (c. 1665–1725) and Mairearad nighean Lachlainn (c. 1660–c. 1755) was collected from "oral tradition in the centuries that followed the Battle of Culloden."[97] Composing in a non-dominant language afforded these poets a measure of secrecy so that they did not need to conceal their political views. An exception to the oral form of this poetry is the manuscript of poems and songs collected by Donnchadh MacRath (Duncan MacRae) of Inverinate entitled "Làmhsgrìobhainn Fheàrnaig" ("Fernaig Manuscript") (see Figure 11).

Consisting of twelve works by MacRath himself plus thirty-seven items by seventeen other poets, the manuscript is "a contemporary manuscript witness in Gaelic" that offers "a clan insider's perspective on developments at the very beginning of Jacobitism," including "the scribe's reaction to the flight of James, the fleeting rejoicing over the victory at Killiecrankie, and the beginning of a yearning for the King over the Water."[98]

In terms of the Irish Gaelic situation, Éamonn Ó Ciardha has analyzed Irish Gaelic poetry circulating at the time of the War of the Two Kings in Ireland "both in manuscript and in the folk tradition" that "illuminate[d] the major events of the war."[99] The diversity of these works, he argues, suggests that "the poetry was being heard by the greater populace. It became a medium whereby news of political and military events percolated down the social pyramid."[100] In the Irish Gaelic literary tradition, Aogán Ó Rathaille popularized the *aisling* genre of poems in which "a poet encounters a vision-woman," an allegorical representative of Ireland, "who foretells a Stuart redeemer."[101] In Ó Rathaille's "Gile na Gile" ("Brightness of Brightness"), for example, the vision-woman informs the poet/narrator:

> Of the prince revisiting where fealty is owed him
> Of the grimmest exile to which evil men forced him
> And of things more fearful still I will leave unspoken.[102]

She helps him escape from the fort where both are imprisoned, but remains in thrall herself "to a horned clown and his doleful breed." The poem concludes with the

---

[97] MacCoinnich, "Clanship."　　[98] MacCoinnich, "Clanship."　　[99] Ó Ciardha, *Ireland*, p. 80.
[100] Ó Ciardha, *Ireland*, p. 80.　　[101] Ó Tuama, *Reposessions*, p. 60.
[102] O'Connor, "*Gile na Gile*."

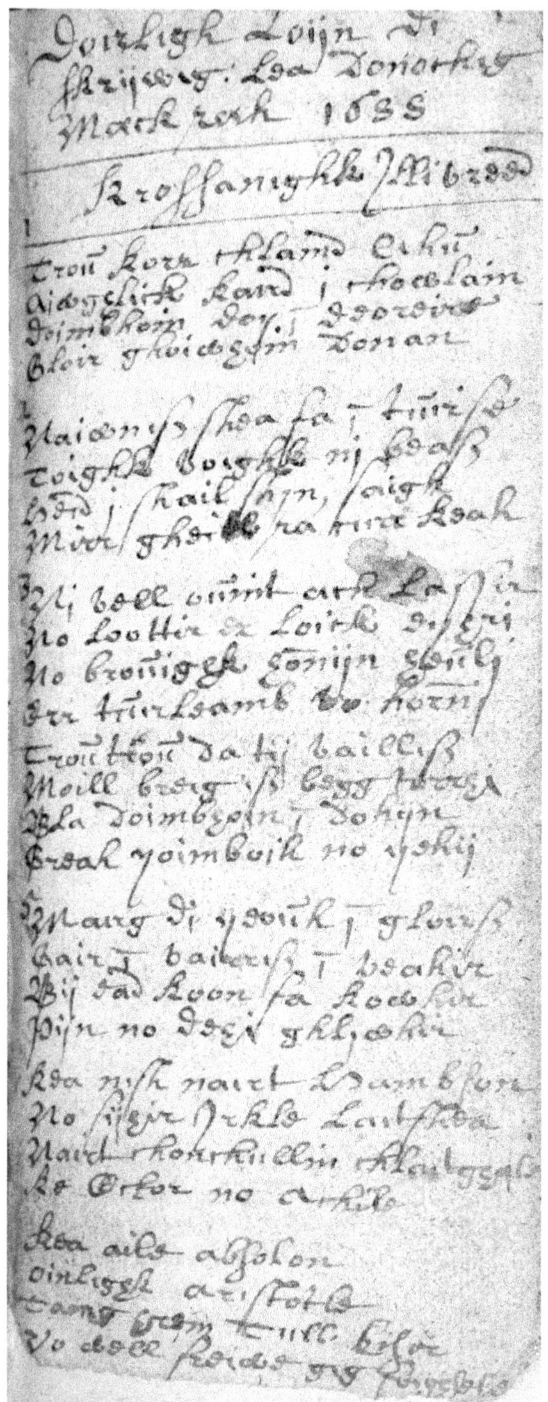

Figure 11 Làmh-sgrìobhainn Fheàrnaig/Fernaig Manuscript. With permission of University of Glasgow Archives & Special Collections. MS Gen 85 cf. https://www.gla.ac.uk/collections/#/details?irn=266199&catType=C

poet/narrator venting his grief that the "Fairest of fair" remains "Without rescue until our heroes come over the sea." As Vincent Morley indicates, "Jacobite compositions from the 1690s and the early decades of the eighteenth century tended to be aristocratic in tone and commonly deplored the death, expropriation or exile of prominent Jacobites."[103] The poetry composed during this era set the template for Irish Gaelic political poetry over the next century, for, as Breandán Ó Buachalla suggests, "Its underlying values, its rhetoric, its ideology can be readily identified as Jacobite; the main poets of the period can be classified as Jacobite poets, that is, poets who championed the cause of James II."[104]

Latin poetry also had a "prominent and distinctive place" in the multinational networks of Jacobitism. As Edward Taylor notes, "Latin's conservative connotations and generic traditions made it particularly useful for expressing Jacobite" themes.[105] James Philp's Latin manuscript poem "Panurgi Philo-Caballi Scoti" ("The Grameid"), for example, celebrates the exploits of Viscount Dundee during the Highland War. Composed originally in 1691, the poem was also copied out numerous times, including an elaborate version done in 1730 (see Figures 12 and 13).

Like Philp's poem, the anonymous 5,500-line "Poema de Hibernia," written in Ireland after the Battle of the Boyne (July 1, 1690), also draws on Lucan's *Pharsalia* for its model of a civil war epic (Figure 14).[106]

According to Jack MacQueen, "After 1688, Latin poetry and Jacobitism became virtually synonymous."[107] In the late seventeenth and early eighteenth centuries, the Edinburgh mathematician, doctor and founder of the Royal College of Physicians Archibald Pitcairne, for example, expressed support for the Stuarts and for the Episcopal Church in Scotland verse in Latin, circulating his works in manuscript form, as printed singles as well as in book form.[108] Pitcairne's poem on John Graham of Claverhouse, "In Mortem Vicecomentis Teodunensis," for example, which connects the death of the Jacobite commander with the end of the Scottish nation, was shared with supporters both in manuscript (Figure 15) and in a cheap paper printed publication known as *Poemata Selecta* (Figure 16):

> Ultime scotorum! Potuit, quo sospite solo,
> libertas patriæ salva fuisse tuæ;
> te moriente novos accepit scotia cives,
> accepitque novos, te moriente, deos.
> Illa tibi superesse negat, tu non potes illi,

---

[103] Morley, "Irish Jacobitism, 1691–1790," p. 36.
[104] Ó Buachalla, "Irish Jacobite Poetry," p. 40.   [105] Taylor, "Jacobites."
[106] See Philp, "Panurgi" and Lenihan and Sidwell.
[107] MacQueen, "From Rome to Ruddiman," p. 203.
[108] Editions of *Poemata Selecta* were printed in 1710, 1727 and 1729.

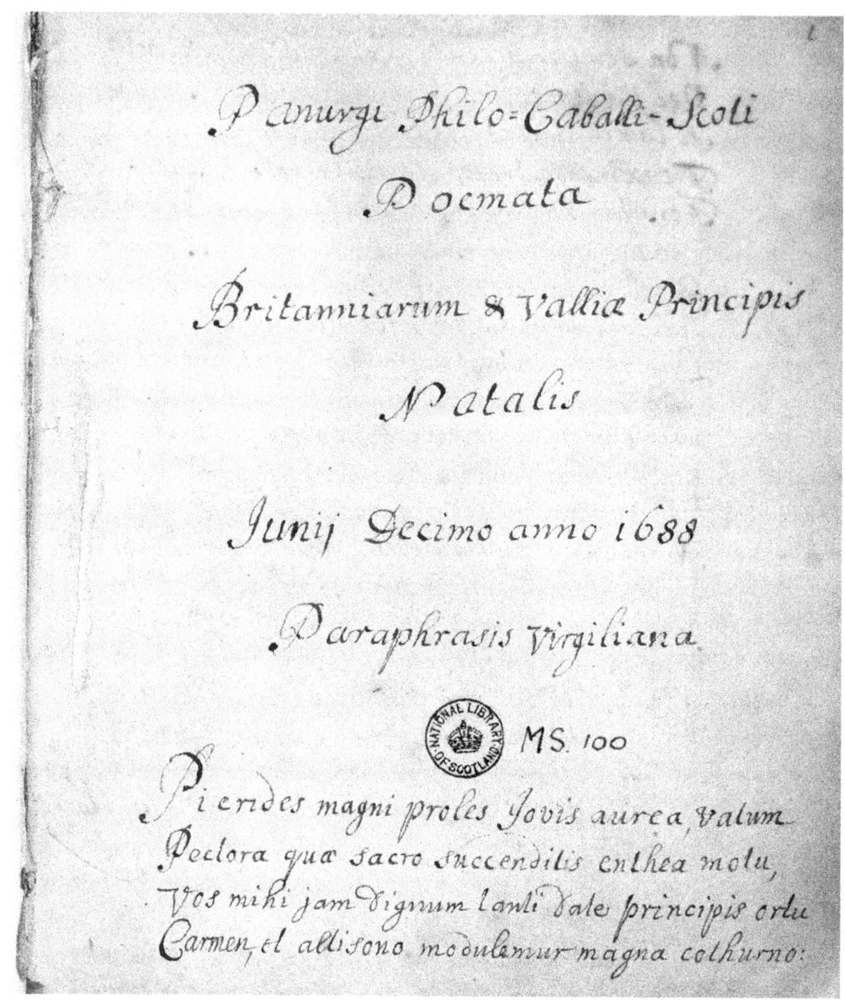

Figure 12 "Panurgi Philo-Cabelli-Scoti Grameidos" (1691). Courtesy of
National Library of Scotland. MS. 100.

Figure 13 "Panurgi Philo-Cabelli-Scoti Grameidos" (1730). Courtesy of National Library of Scotland. MS. 318.

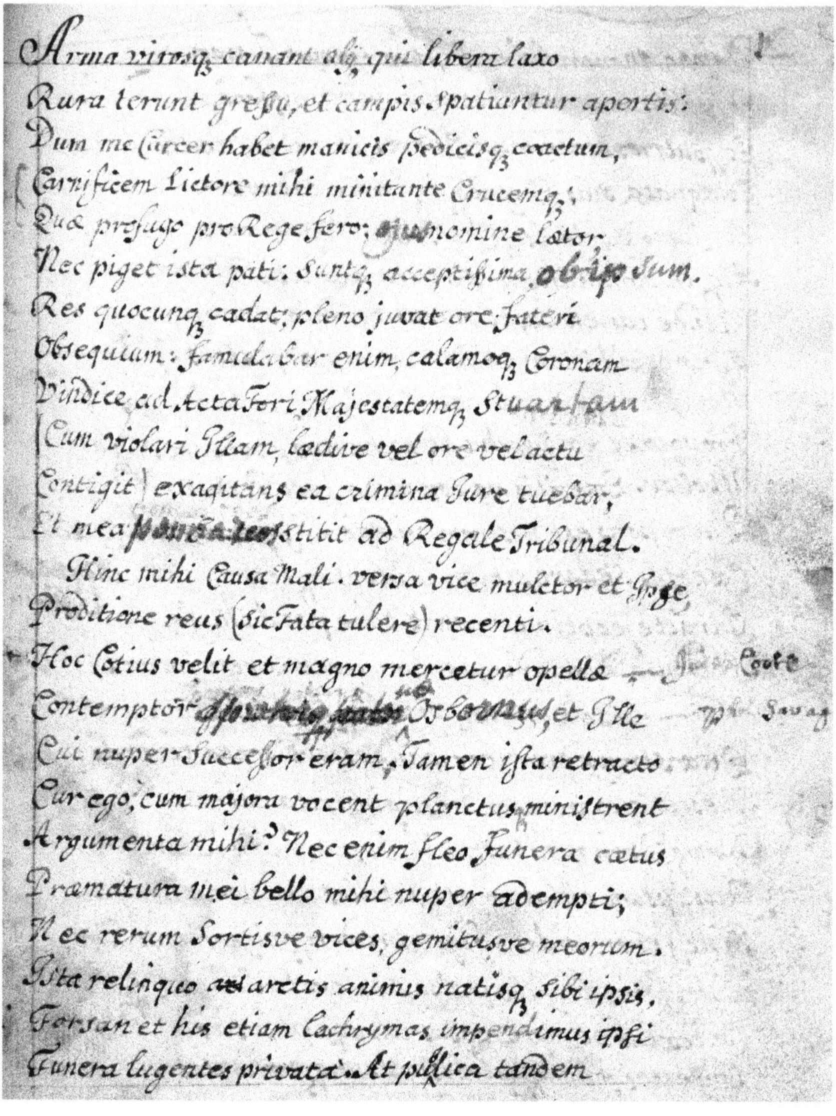

Arma virosq[ue] canant alij, qui libera laxo
Rura terunt gressu, et campis spatiantur apertis:
Dum me Carcer habet manicis pedicisq[ue] coactum,
Carnificem Lictore mihi minitante Crucemq[ue];
Quâ profugo pro Rege fero; nomine lator;
Nec piget ista pati. Suntq[ue] acceptissima obsijo Sum.
Res quocunq[ue] cadat; pleno juvat ore fateri
Obsequium: famulabar enim, calamoq[ue] Coronam
Vindice ad Acta Fori Majestatemq[ue] Stuartam
Cum violari Illam, lædive vel ore vel actu
Contigit) exagitans ea crimina Jure tuebar;
Et mea ... stitit ad Regale Tribunal.
　　Hinc mihi Causa Mali. versa vice mulctor et Ipse,
Proditione reus (sic Fata tulere) recenti.
Hoc Cotius velit et magno mercetur opella ...
Contemptor ... Orbonsus, et Ille ...
Cui nuper Successor eram, Tamen ista retracto.
Cur ego, cum majora vocent planctus ministrent
Argumenta mihi? Nec enim fleo funera cætus
Præmatura mei bello mihi nuper adempti;
Nec rerum Sortisve vices, gemitusve meorum.
Ista relinquo ... arctis animis natisq[ue] sibi ipsis,
Forsan et his etiam lachrymas impendimus ipsi
Funera lugentes privatâ. At publica tandem

Figure 14 "Poema de Hibernia." Gilbert Ms 141. f. 1. Courtesy of Dublin City Library & Archive.

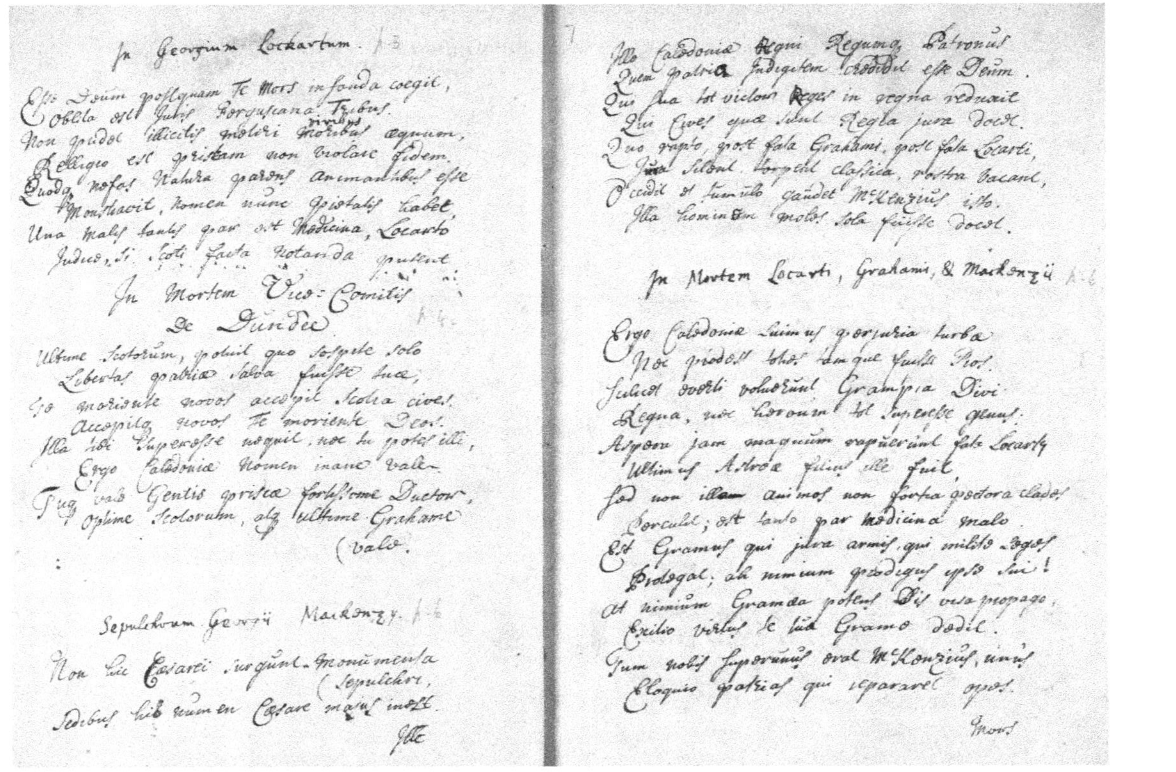

Figure 15 Archibald Pitcairne. "In mortem Vice Comitis De Dundee." Catalogus Librorum Archibald Pitcairne. pp. 6–7. Courtesy of the University of Edinburgh, Heritage Collections.

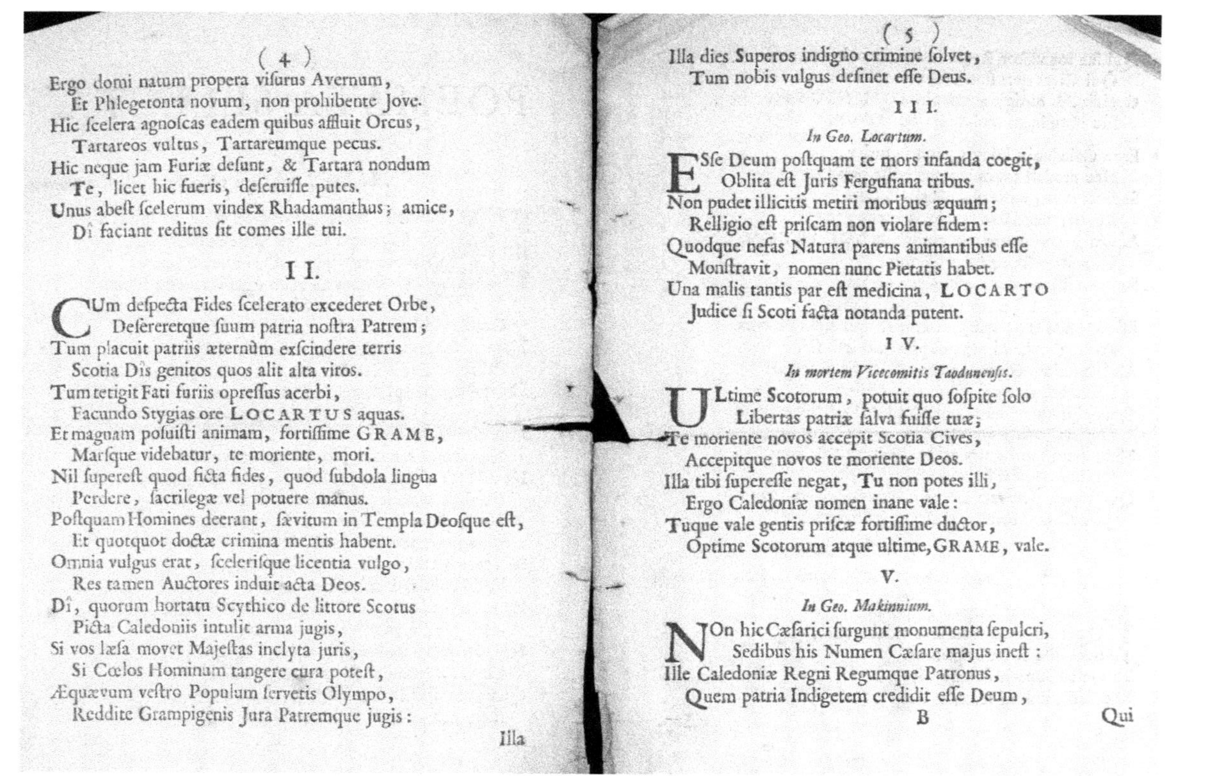

Figure 16 Archibald Pitcairne. "VI: In mortem Vicecomitis Taodunensis." *Poemata Selecta*. La.III.629. p. 5. Courtesy of the University of Edinburgh, Heritage Collections.

> ergo caledoniæ nomen inane, vale!
> tuque vale, gentis priscæ fortissime ductor,
> *Ultime Scotorum atque optime, Grame, Vale.*[109]

Pitcairne died in 1713, but his son would go on to join the next major military Jacobite rising in 1715. Pitcairne's literary contribution to Jacobite counter-memory would also live on as his poem on Dundee found its way to John Dryden who translated and published it, among other places, in *The Fifth Part of Miscellany poems. Containing Variety of New Translations of the Ancient Poets: Together with Several Original Poems* (1716):

> Oh last and best of *Scots*: who didst maintain
> Thy Country's Freedom, from a foreign Reign;
> New People fill the Land now thou art gone,
> New Gods the Temples, and new Kings the Throne.
> *Scotland* and Thee did each in other live;
> Nor would'st thou her, nor could she thee survive.
> Farewel, who, dying, didst support the State,
> And couldst not fall but with thy Country's Fate.

Pitcairne's (and Dryden's) representation of a fallen nation whose gods and kings had been replaced in the temples and on the throne by foreigners would prove a pervasive cultural memory for the Jacobites over the next decades, serving either as a tragic narrative, or, when combined with a providential belief in a promised restoration after such a fall, as a powerful metaphor of hope.

2.4 Recollecting and Re-collecting the Jacobites in 1715

If the 1688 Revolution constituted an extraordinary intervention on the part of a foreign leader to assume governance over England, Scotland and Ireland, Queen Anne's choice to name a German prince, George of Hanover, as heir to the crowns of Britain and Ireland after her death must be seen as equally as extraordinary. In fact, Ronald G. Asch suggests that "the Hanoverian claims to the crown (although based on the Act of Settlement of 1701) were even more controversial than those of William and Mary and Queen Anne, as the Hanoverians were only distantly related to the royal dynasty."[110] Anne's decision resulted in the disqualification of over fifty relations who were closer by ties of blood but who were Catholic. To draw attention away from the particulars of this settlement, supporters of the new dynasty were eager to represent the

---

[109] See Corp, *A Court in Exile*, p. 222. Williams points out that Pitcairne's poems emphasize the connection between the Stuart monarchs and the seasonal calendar of the Episcopal Church, emphasizing the spiritual and natural interconnections of Jacobite culture ("Archibald Pitcairne's Liturgical Year").

[110] Asch, "Hanoverian Monarchy," p. 25.

new monarch as the fulfilment of the events begun in 1688. Aston and Bankhurst note that "One of the most common patterns was to associate the arrival of the new dynasty with the continued march of progress. Following on from the Glorious Revolution, the Hanoverians were viewed as having a particular role to play in the providential history of the nation."[111]

For Jacobite supporters, however, the accession of yet another foreign monarch to the thrones of Britain and Ireland offered an opportunity to generate support for a new armed attempt to restore the Stuarts. In fact, the event that became known as the 1715 Jacobite rising unfolded in various locations in both England and Scotland. While the government was able to arrest Jacobite leaders in southern and western England before armed conflict broke out, there was military activity in "northern, central and western Scotland; Lowlands and Borders Scotland; and northern England," as Daniel Szechi notes.[112] The Jacobites in Scotland under John Erskine, Lord Mar, amassed a sizeable army and gained considerable ground. An indeterminate battle at Sherriffmuir on November 15, 1715, however, left the Jacobites unmoored. By the time that James Francis Edward Stuart landed in Scotland in December 1715, the Jacobite troops were diminished, and foreign soldiers were arriving to support the government forces. By February, James had returned to France and the Hanoverian forces had suppressed what remained of the rising. Margaret Sankey comments on the British government's mixed strategy in the aftermath of the 1715. As Sankey indicates, "George I and his government had to tailor their reaction to the rebellion in such a way that it effectively discouraged further participation in Jacobite insurgency, undercut the rebels' ability to challenge the state, and made clear the regime's intention to use a firm hand at preventing rebellion." At the same time, however, she notes, the government needed to avoid the appearance of acting in too draconian a manner, thus alienating both the general population that they were trying to win over as well as "powerful magnates likely to petition for the lives of captured rebels."[113]

The events of 1715 and 1716 were represented in the rapidly expanding periodical press that developed in the aftermath of the lapse of the Licensing Act in 1695. Commenting in 1712 upon the "furious itch of novelty" which generated a taste for news, the *British Mercury* describes an "inundation of *Postmen, Postboys, Evening Posts, Supplements, Daily Courants* and *Protestant Post Boys*, amounting to twenty-one every week, besides many more which have not survived to this time, and besides the [*London*] *Gazette*, which has the sanction of public authority."[114] Newspapers took on the role of

---

[111] Aston and Bankhurst, *Negotiating Toleration*, p. 6. See also Sirota and MacInnes, *The Hanoverian Succession in Great Britain*.

[112] Szechi, *1715*, p. 5.   [113] Sankey, *Jacobite Prisoners*.

[114] Quoted in Cranfield, *Development*, pp. 9–10.

providing an up to date account of the actions that were taking place around Britain during the conflict, moving to displace the previous authority of manuscript news in the mediascape. The effect of the newspapers on readers was mixed, however. On the one hand, they printed assertions of loyalty from locations in Britain, generating a sense of an imagined community of supporters for the Hanoverian regime. On the other hand, newspapers put the ongoing conflict taking place on British shores right before the eyes of the reading public, making the details of this internal conflict visible to more people than had ever consumed news before.[115]

In addition to the new newspapers that came into existence in 1715 and 1716, new periodical essays such as Joseph Addison's *The Free-Holder* and Richard Steele's *The Town Talk* appeared in the late 1715 and early 1716 to manage the information that was being circulated in the papers. Rejecting what they termed the "impertinencies" of the "authors of daily or weekly papers" who spread "errors among the rest of the people," Addison and Steele repackaged recent events in such a way as to retroactively minimize the recent threat to the government.[116] By representing their editorial avatars in their periodical essays as the voices of "common Sense" and taste, they steered readers toward viewing the accession of George I as the only way to save the British nation and the "Civil Liberties," rights and property of its subjects.[117]

During the conflict and its immediate aftermath, adherents of both sides expressed their concerns for the future of their country in printed works at numerous price points designed to circulate amongst readers of a variety of ranks. The pro-Hanoverian "An Imitation of the Prophecy of Nereus" by Thomas Tickell, which was published both as a cheap broadsheet (Figure 17) and in more expensive pamphlet form in 1715, satirizes the Earl of Mar by representing him as "aged Wizard" who leads a group of "hungry Mountaineers" who are "Inflam'd with Bag-pipe and with Brandy":

> What boots thy high-born Host of Beggars.
> *Macleans, Mackenzies,* and *Macgrigors,*
> With *Popish* Cut-throats, perjur'd Ruffians,
> And *Forster's* Troop of Ragamuffins?[118]

The wizard foresees a temporary success for James ("Three Moons thy *Jemmy* shall command,/With Highland Scepter in his hand") but pronounces that the ultimate victory is "decreed" for the reign of George: "Heav'n shall for ever on Him smile." Although the poem criticizes Mar for betraying the

---

[115] See also Hagan, "Reading the News"; and Harris, *Revolution*.
[116] Steele, *Town Talk*, p. 79.　　　[117] Addison, *Free-Holder*, p. 38; p. 9.
[118] "An Imitation of The Prophecy of Nereus."

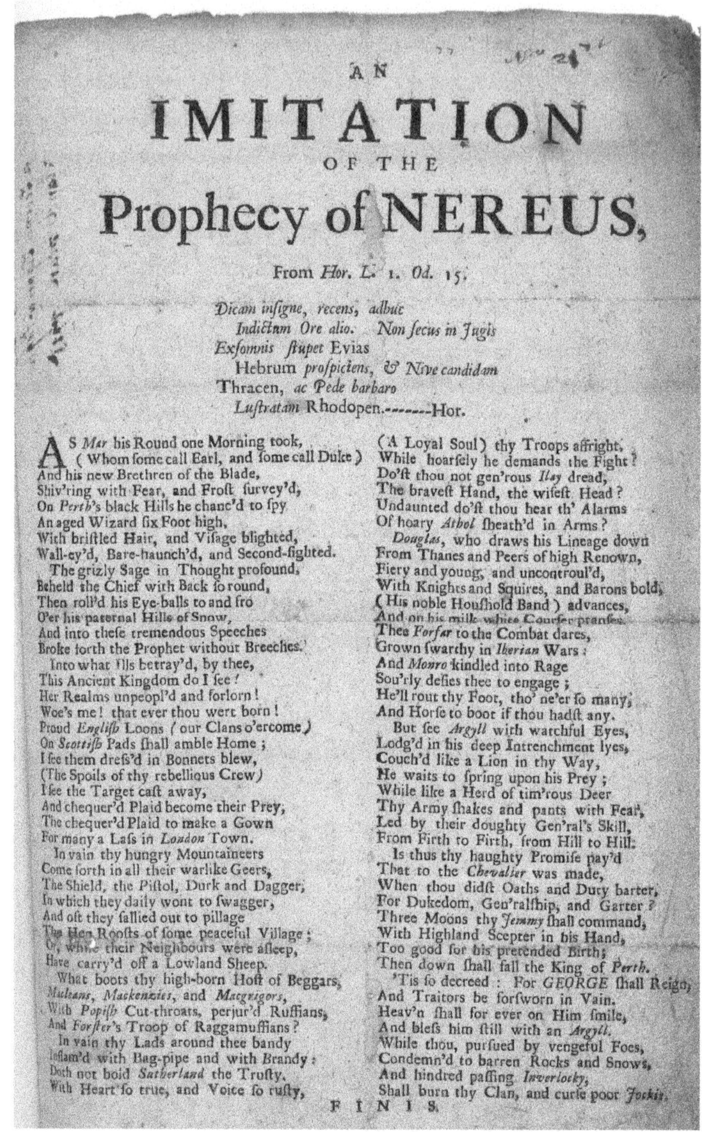

Figure 17 "An Imitation of the Prophecy of Nereus," Papers Concerning the Jacobite Rebellion, Vol. 1. Courtesy of National Library of Scotland, MS.487. f77.

"Ancient Kingdom" of Scotland, it also demonstrates its own anti-Highland sentiment by drawing on negative stereotypes of Highlanders, even representing the wizard himself as a "Prophet without Breeches" who is "Wall-ey'd, Bare-haunch'd, and Second-sighted."

Another broadside entitled "An Excellent new Song lately composed to the Tune of the bonny Broom," on the other hand, offers a Jacobite perspective couched within a work that can be read as loyal to the Hanoverian cause. The song in printed form begins from the perspective of a Jacobite narrator who laments the "Hard Fate" that he is banished and labeled a "Rebel" because he serves "the bravest Prince/that ever yet was Born." The narrator articulates a longing for the "King" to return again: "then would my Heart rejoice." Until that, the narrator suggests, "old *Calidon*" will know nothing but "Grief and Care." This first part of the printed song corresponds to a song in manuscript entitled "To the Tune of The broom of Codon [sic] knowes" that appears in a "Collection of MS Poems Chiefly Scotch, with a few in Latin" housed in the University of Edinburgh's Special Collections (see Figure 18).

In the printed version of the song, however, a section entitled "An ANSWER to the above Lines" appears after the first part, in which a different narrative voice confirms a government perspective, suggesting that "happy Days and Peace" in Scotland can only happen when "King *George*" is "fix[ed]" "upon the Throne" (see Figure 19).

This narrator imagines the Hanoverian settlement as a seamless dynastic connection with George taking the place "of his Ancestors old" and with supporters who fight for him "Like Old *Scots* men of Weir [War]." From this perspective, it is James who is the foreigner, as the narrator imagines "that Romish Prince,/that would us sore down-hold" being banished from the kingdom. Although "An Excellent new Song" concludes with verses representing a narrator who supports the Hanoverian succession, the chorus that that appears in full at the very end of the song reinforces the sentiments of loss and displacement associated with a Jacobite rather than a Hanoverian worldview:

> *O the B[r]oom the bonny bony Broom,*
> *The Broom of* Colding-Knows
> *O if I were at home again.*
> *Amongst my Country Hows.*[119]

It is difficult to know the exact connection between the manuscript and the printed versions of the song. Did the former Jacobite version predate the printed version or did a Jacobite supporter (or a later collector of Jacobite materials) write out the relevant section of the song after having read a printed version? Regardless of the temporal relationship between the two, the case of this song serves as a pertinent example of the knotted cultural memories that are the focus of this investigation.

---

[119] "An Excellent New Song Lately Composed." Pittock suggests that "well-known songs such as 'The Broom of Cowdenknowes' were turned to Jacobite purposes" ("Scottish Song," p. 108).

Figure 18 "To the Tune of The broom of Codon [sic] knows," "Collection of MS Poems Chiefly Scotch," with a few in Latin.: La.II.358. f.173 v. Courtesy of The University of Edinburgh, Heritage Collections.

Also important in shaping the way in which "the '15" would be remembered are the popular histories that were published in the wake of the suppression of the rising such as the anonymous *A Compleat History of the Late Rebellion* (1716), Robert Patten's *The History of the Late Rebellion* (1717) and Peter Rae's *The History of the Late Rebellion* (1718). All three of these popular

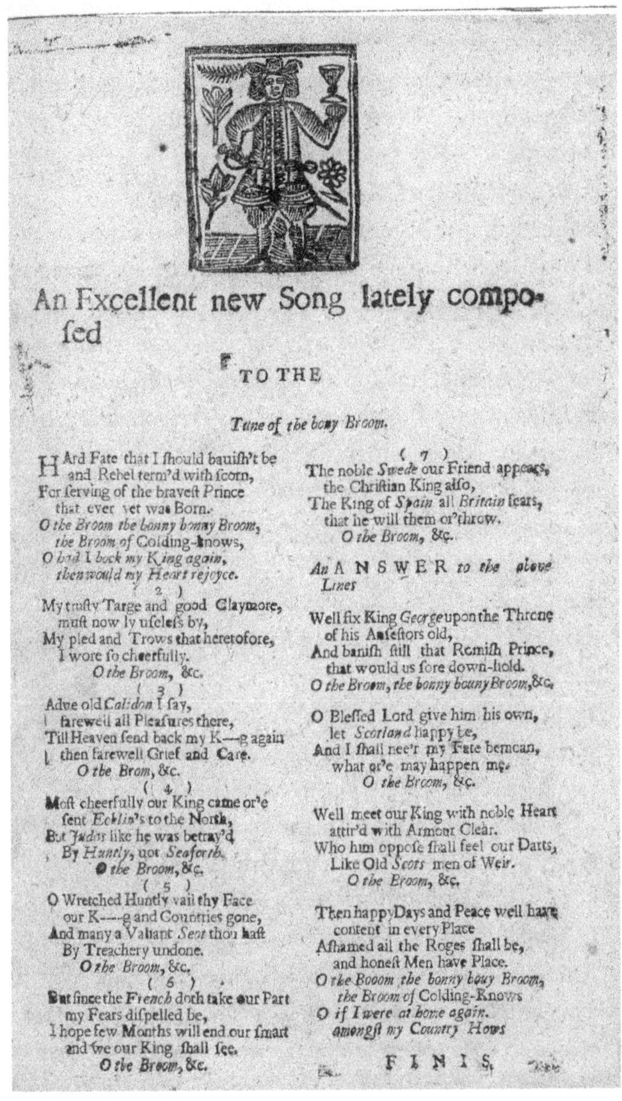

An Excellent new Song lately composed

TO THE

Tune of the bony Broom.

HArd Fate that I should banish't be
　and Rebel term'd with scorn,
For serving of the bravest Prince
　that ever yet was Born.
O the Broom the bonny bonny Broom,
　the Broom of Colding-knows,
O had I bock my King again,
　then would my Heart rejoyce.
　　(2)
My trusty Targe and good Claymore,
　must now ly useless by,
My pled and Trows that heretofore,
　I wore so cheerfully.
　　O the Broom, &c.
　　(3)
Adue old *Calidon* I say,
　farewell all Pleasures there,
Till Heaven send back my K——g again
　then farewell Grief and Care.
　　O the Brom, &c.
　　(4)
Most cheerfully our King came or'e
　sent *Ecklin's* to the North,
But *Judos* like he was betray'd
　By *Huntly,* not *Seaforth.*
　　O the Broom, &c.
　　(5)
O Wretched Huntly vail thy Face
　our K——g and Countries gone,
And many a Valiant *Scot* thou hast
　By Treachery undone.
　　O the Broom, &c.
　　(6)
But since the *French* doth take our Part
　my Fears dispelled be,
I hope few Months will end our smart
　and we our King shall see.
　　O the Broom, &c.

　　(7)
The noble *Swede* our Friend appears,
　the Christian King also,
The King of *Spain* all *Britain* fears,
　that he will them or'throw.
　　O the Broom, &c.

An ANSWER *to the above
Lines*

Well fix King *George* upon the Throne
　of his Ansestors old,
And banish still that Romish Prince,
　that would us sore down-hold.
O the Broom, the bonny bouny Broom, &c.

O Blessed Lord give him his own,
　let *Scotland* happy be,
And I shall nee'r my Fate bemoan,
　what or'e may happen me.
　　O the Broom, &c.

Well meet our King with noble Heart
　attir'd with Armour Clear.
Who him oppose shall feel our Darts,
　Like Old *Scots* men of Weir.
　　O the Broom, &c.

Then happy Days and Peace well have
　content in every Place
Ashamed all the Roges shall be,
　and honest Men have Place.
O the Booom the bonny bouy Broom,
　the Broom of Colding-Knows
O if I were at home again.
　amongst my Country Hows

FINIS.

Figure 19 "An Excellent New Song lately Composed," Jacobite Relics MS. 2960 f. 88. Courtesy of National Library of Scotland.

histories used information that originally appeared in the newspapers, sometimes re-printing it verbatim. But they also shaped that information into
a narrative arc that represented the 1715 rising as a brief incident on a wide
horizon of peace and prosperity. As Ann Rigney suggests, "events do not
'naturally' take the form of a story, meaning that whoever narrates events is
in fact involved in actively shaping experience into an intelligible pattern with

a beginning, middle and end, and with an economy of antipathy and sympathy centered on particular human figures." By suggesting that "the very Arm of the *Almighty* manifestly engag'd to assert the Cause of his Church, in the Defeat and Infatuation of her Enemies," for example, the author of *A Compleat History* implicitly asserts that the outcome of the 1715 rising was predetermined by a Providence that supports the Hanoverian succession.[120]

At the same time, popular histories such as these also inadvertently worked to keep traces of pro-Jacobite perspectives in circulation. In its efforts to offer as "compleat" as possible an account, *A Compleat History*, for example, reprints Jacobite material such as the "Manifesto *by the Noblemen, Gentlemen and others who dutifully appear at this* Time" which asserts *"the undoubted Right of their Lawful Sovereign*, James *the* Eighth" and attacks the supporters of George I.[121] Patten and Rae, too, include documents relating to both sides of the conflict, with Patten (a former Jacobite captured at Preston who subsequently turned King's evidence) also presenting a sympathetic account of the "unfortunate Jacobite Gentlemen," including a positive view of Lord Derwentwater, one of the two peers who was executed. The publication of speeches of executed Jacobites such as James Shepheard during this time period (Figure 20) suggests a similar ambiguous appeal to both Jacobite and non-Jacobite audiences.

More overtly coded Jacobite perspectives continued to be published in the years between the 1715 and 1745 risings, especially in Scotland, by cultural figures such as Allan Ramsay. Ramsay dedicated *The Ever Green, Being a Collection of Scots Poems, Wrote by the Ingenious Before 1600* (1724), for example, to the pro-Jacobite Duke of Hamilton and the Royal Company of Archers, while his successful *The Gentle Shepherd* (1725) masks Jacobite sympathies by focusing on an earlier Stuart restoration, that of Charles II. Many Scots Gaelic poets also maintained their adherence to the Jacobite cause.[122] Other Scottish poets such as James Thomson (a Scot who relocated to London), however, asserted their allegiance to the Hanoverian dynasty and attempted to knit the British nation together in such works as *Britannia, a Poem* (1729) and *The Seasons* (1730) by re-envisioning a collective past and future.

Such a mythic knitting together necessitated disregarding the situation of Ireland which by this time was burdened by additional Penal Laws, with the Declaratory Act of 1719 asserting the right of the Parliament of Great Britain to make laws for Ireland. Ó Tuama notes that "For want of patronage during the eighteenth century, [Gaelic] poets increasingly became wandering teachers, musicians or labourers, and fell more frequently into poverty," but they

---

[120] Rigney, "Dynamics," p. 347. A Compleat History, p. 2.

[121] *A Compleat History of the Late Rebellion.* London, 1716, p. 18.

[122] Stiùbhart, "Adaptation,"

The Dying

SPEECH

OF

JAMES SHEPHEARD;

Who Suffer'd Death at T Y B U R N, *March* the 17th, 17$\frac{17}{18}$.
Deliver'd by him to the Sheriff, at the Place of Execution.

I AM brought hither by the Almighty's Permission and the Usurper's Power, to whose Tyranny I thought to put an End, in order to facilitate my Lawful Sovereign's Return, and shorten the tedious Havock of a Civil War.

Whether the Principle on which I had conceiv'd this Deliverance to my Country, and Justice to my SOVEREIGN be really and strictly defensible or not, let who will canvass for me, tho' I can't help thinking, that if all and every Subject of these Realms were truly sensible of the Wrongs of their Prince and Country, the Reproach to their Faith, and the Disgrace to the *British* Name, and were as deeply touch'd with them as I am, I should then depart with an universal Approbation of my Countrymen, as I do with an absolute Perswasion of the Honesty and publick Spiritedness of my Intention.

As for those who are otherwise minded, who can help it ; it would be lost Labour to contend with them. I shall therefore only give the World the true Motives which at first engaged me : And tho' they will not take with every Humour, and every Interest, yet am I well assured they will justify me thro' my dear SAVIOUR's Merits at his Righteous Bar, whether I am now going.

Where, but in my own Country , (O Blessed God receive me from it !) has a publick National Price been twice set on the Head of its Lawful Sovereign ? And this by the Protestant Invaders of his, and his Subject's undoubted Rights : And can all this full length of Villany be allowed to such Invaders ? And an hearty Subject to his Injur'd Prince not be allow'd, in vertue of his Allegiance, to strike the Ravager, let Equity itself pronounce.

The Earl of *Peterborough*'s doubtful Message, I forbear to insist upon, because as yet it may be doubtful, the Hand of Time will clear it : But who can be Criminal to suspect an *Usurper* of Murder, the Sin that so easily besets him, and so well befits him ? His destroying and reducing to Beggery those Gentlemen, with their Families, whom his General had receiv'd to Mercy, shews his utter want of any Notion of Honour, or Spirit, to Grace the Throne he has Usurp'd.

To invade the RIGHTS of a CHURCH, which he came chiefly on *Pretence of defending*, and of which he *feigns* himself a Member, is a prime Instance of his *Bangorian* Sincerity.

In short, to manage by Corruption, and barter away a brave People's Rights with their own Cash, to Rule a Nation with a Rod of Iron, and Rein it with a Halter, are strong lines of Government for the squeamish Constitution of *BRITONS*; and let this close the Character.

If these are Princely Qualities, and denote the true Vicegerent of Heaven, let the *British Annals* brand me.

I die a sincere, tho' an unworthy Member of the *CHURCH of ENGLAND, as it stood before the Revolution*, and from that *CHURCH*, her Articles, Liturgies and Homilies I have learned to abhor all KING KILLING *and deposing* DOCTRINES : What the adherers of this Government may think of this Asseveration, is the least of my Concern ; I have only now to beg of the Almighty, my dear Redeemer, to pardon my Weakness in prescribing Means of his All-wise Providence and JUSTICE.

I now desire all, whom I have any way offended, to forgive me ; but more particularly I ask pardon of the Reverend Mr. *Leak, and all his Brethren*, for my Rashness in supposing that he, or any of them, (who are all Strangers to me) could take Satisfaction in any sort of Revenge (tho' a just one) on the Guilty.

And here I think it proper to declare, that I never received any Instructions from, or ever heard any thing of my Master, the Reverend Mr. *Hale*, tending to, or countenancing a dislike of this Government.

May it Please the Almighty to accept my earnest Desire to serve my Country ; may he be Pleas'd to bless this Land, and *its Rightful King,* JAMES *the Third* ; may he grant him a speedy *Restoration*, and happy Issue from his Body, and a *Glorious Reign :* And Lastly, may he of his Infinite Goodness, and for the Sake of the Ever-Blessed *Jesus*, my Redeemer, receive me to his Mercy and Everlasting Rest.

O Lord ! into thy Hands I commend my Spirit, Come, Lord Jesus, come quickly. Amen.

P. S. The World may please to take Notice, that no Allowance was any Way made to my plain Intimation in the Letter, that I wanted Authority and Commission, from my *Lawful Sovereign*, to have put what I had conceived, in Execution ; and that I had projected, first, to obtain such a Commission without which (the Intimation is strong) I intended not to act ; so that if they on the Bench had *any Candour*, there was apparent Room to have shewn it.

But I have since learn'd that such a Commission would never be granted, being fully inform'd and assured, since my Confinement, that the KING has always disclaimed such Attempts, and in his *DECLARATION*, upon his going to *Scotland*, expresly forbad any such ; which makes me, in the first Place, admire *at the Greatness and Goodness of my* PRINCE *(the distinguishing, full, Mark of his Family)* amidst so many Wrongs, and then regret my Ignorance of that Particular in his DECLARATION.

J A M E S S H E P H E A R D.

Figure 20 "The dying speech of James Shepheard: who suffer'd death at Tyburn, March the 17th, 1717–18; Deliver'd by him to the sheriff, at the place of execution." Courtesy of Harvard Law School Library, Historical & Special Collections.

continued to compose "with extraordinary virtuosity within the norms of the traditional aristocratic literary tradition."[123] Ó Ciardha comments on the "Irish Jacobite despair in the late 1720s" in the work of Gaelic poets such *as* Pádraig Ó Suilleabháin and Seán na Ráithíneach Ó Murchú/Murchadha, even though, on the continent, there was "a heroic literary tradition of the Irish Brigades" that lasted until the end of the Seven Year's War.[124] He notes, however, that "dormant Jacobite spirits in Ireland and on the continent revived with the outbreak of [the War of Jenkins' Ear] in 1739."[125] The appearance of Charles Edward Stuart on the remote island of Eriskay in July 1745, and the subsequent amassing of the Jacobite army provided new inspiration for Jacobite creatives in all literary traditions.

2.5 Re-presenting the Jacobites in 1745

The 1745 rising was originally intended to include French support, but interception by British forces meant that Charles arrived in Scotland accompanied only by a small band of followers. Over the course of the summer and fall, however, after raising James Stuart's standard at Glenfinnan, the Jacobite army grew in strength, occupying Edinburgh, gaining a significant victory over the government troops at Prestonpans on September 21, 1745, and preparing to march down to London. As during the earlier conflict, newspapers helped keep the population abreast of the events as they were unfolding. The number of newspapers and other periodicals in circulation had increased steeply since the 1715 rising, however. Bob Harris estimates that in 1745 there were eighteen papers produced in London ("eight weeklies, four thrice-weekly evening papers and six dailies"); approximately forty papers in other English locations; and four newspapers produced in Scotland.[126] Moreover, the significant shift in the mediascape to a more print-saturated environment that had taken place over the previous decades had generated a more self-conscious discourse regarding the effect of consuming printed works. As Harris writes, during the time from late September to early December, "the demand, the anxiety for news and for information reached an intensity that was probably unparalleled for the whole of the century."[127] Not only were more writers and other public figures concerned about the potential impact of "fake news" on the British population's understanding of the conflict and their ensuing attitude to events, but there was also increasing concern about the correct way to read and consume news. A pamphlet entitled *Seasonable Considerations on the Present War in Scotland* warns of the problems that occur when readers don't take

---

[123] Ó Tuama, *Reposessions*, p. 128.
[124] Ó Ciardha, *Ireland and the Jacobite Cause*, pp. 260–261.
[125] Ó Ciardha, *Ireland and the Jacobite Cause*, p. 271.   [126] Harris, "Great Palladium," p. 68.
[127] Harris, "Great Palladium," p. 68.

news seriously enough. It notes that at first the rising "was looked at as a Thing below Notice, and for several Weeks People were in doubt here, whether there was any Rising in that Country at all."[128] The author suggests that this initial dismissal was replaced by a heightened sense of panic with "the marching of a Body of 4000 Men down to *Edinburgh*" and "the Defeat of General *Cope*" at Prestonpans.[129] This sense of alarm also made the reading population more afraid of the Jacobites, raising "the Credit of the *Highlanders* so much, that from being a low and despicable Rabble, they swell'd of a sudden into daring and intrepid Troops, which Character they chiefly derived from the Reports of those whom they had defeated."[130]

While the newspapers were reporting on events from the government's side, Jacobites took advantage of their successes in the early months of the rising to circulate (both orally and in print) materials representing the advantages of their cause for the nations of Scotland, England and Ireland. Charles Edward Stuart's declaration "Unto His Majesty's Subjects" which was read out on October 10, 1745, from Holyrood Palace indicates that the publication of such materials was essential to counteract the accusations of "Popery, Slavery, Tyranny and arbitrary Power" that were being leveled at the Jacobites not only from the "weekly Papers" but also from the pulpits of the clergy (see Figure 21).[131]

Addressing "All His Majesty's Subjects," the declaration sets out to dispel "that Cloud, which the assiduous Pens of ill designing Men have all along, but chiefly now, been endeavouring to cast on the Truth."[132] The Jacobite version of "the Truth" includes condemning the increased taxes and the corruption that has taken place under the "Usurper," as well as questioning whether the new monarch has been able to equal the affective bond offered by "my royal Fore-fathers." The document also registers an understanding of the importance of cultural memory, suggesting that the point of the anti-Jacobite rhetoric is to amplify the negative memories of the Stuarts so that "the real Sense of the Nation's present Sufferings" does not "blot out the Remembrance of past Misfortunes, and of the Outcries formerly raised against the Royal Family." It acknowledges the "Miscarriages" of Charles's grandfather but asserts that "they have been more than atoned for since then" and that the nation now has a chance to learn from its past mistakes and be "secured against the like for the Future."[133]

The Jacobite army traveled into England, seizing Carlisle and marching as far south as Derby, 120 miles from London. On December 6, 1745, however, after receiving incorrect intelligence about the movements of the British army, Charles and his advisors made the decision to return to Scotland. Although

---

[128] *Seasonable Considerations*, p. 3.　　[129] *Seasonable Considerations*, p. 3.
[130] *Seasonable Considerations*, p. 3.　　[131] Charles, *Jacobite Relics*, p. 2.
[132] Charles, *Jacobite Relics*, p. 2.　　[133] "Charles, P.R.," p. 3.

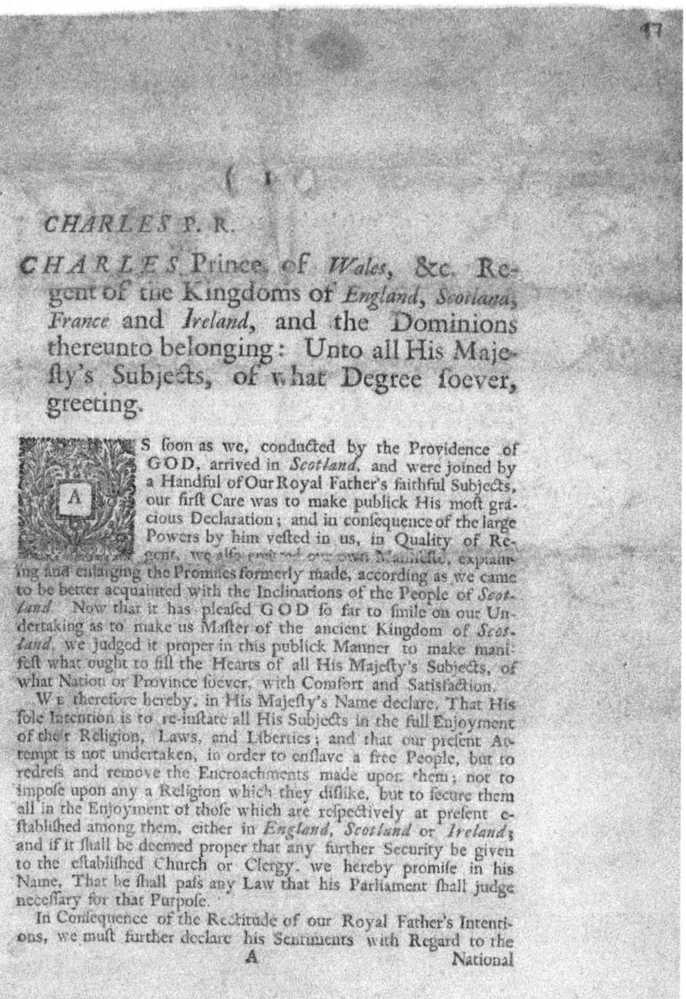

Figure 21 Charles P.R. Jacobite Relics. MS. 2960. f. 97 r. Courtesy of National
Library of Scotland.

they enjoyed a victory at Falkirk on January 17, 1746, the Jacobites retreated
still further north. A night attack on the Duke of Cumberland's forces at Nairn
planned for April 15, 1746 failed miserably, and the exhausted Jacobite army
was defeated at the Battle of Culloden the following day. Charles Edward
Stuart, escaped, however, and, with the help of numerous loyal followers and
local guides, spent the next five months evading government troops. He eventually escaped to France on September 20, 1746.

The suppression of the Jacobite soldiers as well as those who supported (or
were suspected of supporting) them was brutal. Over 3,000 men, women and

children were arrested in the aftermath of the rising.[134] Jails throughout Scotland and parts of England were overflowing, while many prisoners languished on prison ships. Because so many prisoners required processing through the legal system, a lottery system was established whereby only one out of every twenty went to trial; the remainder were transported.[135] Of those who underwent trial, more than 130 were found guilty of treason and sentenced to hanging, drawing and quartering. Four Jacobite peers were also tried for their actions in the rising. George Mackenzie, 3rd Earl of Cromartie was pardoned by the king. William Boyd, 4th Earl of Kilmarnock, and Arthur Elphinstone, Lord Balmerino, were publicly beheaded on Tower Hill in August 1746, and Simon Fraser, Lord Lovat, suffered the same fate in April 1747. Figure 22 represents a popular print of "The Execution of the Earl of Kilmarnock and Lord Balmerino," showing the scene of execution with a view of the Tower of London where the two peers had been held during their trial and sentencing. Like the execution speech of James Shepheard, such printed representations could also serve Jacobite adherents as memorials of those who suffered for their cause.

In addition to seeking the punishment of rebellious bodies, the government also introduced legislation designed to break up the clan system in the Highlands which was considered partially responsible for the fact that so many in the Scottish Highlands took up arms. The 1746 Act of Proscription reinforced the measures passed in the 1716 Disarming Act, adding legislation prohibiting the wearing of Highland clothing. The Heritable Jurisdictions Act (1746) abolished the traditional Highland clan justice system in a professed attempt to render "the Union of the Two Kingdoms more complete."[136] The claim of such a "rendering" of union was counteracted by the fact that, as Murray Pittock notes, Scotland remained a heavily militarized zone for years after the 1745 rising.

The suppression of the Jacobite rising generated celebrations by Hanoverian supporters throughout Britain. But soon after, reports started circulating in London about the brutal behavior of the government troops after Culloden, prompting Tory adherents to apply the epithet "the Butcher" to the Duke of Cumberland.[137] The aftermath of the 1745 rising also saw the publication of numerous printed works designed to establish a pro-government narrative. This was particularly important given the controversy surrounding the victory. As in 1716, many of these pro-government works drew on material originally printed in newspapers. While the newspapers provided information in periodic

---

[134] See Seton and Arnot, *Prisoners*; and The Jacobite Database of 1745.
[135] Seton and Arnot, *Prisoners*, p. 8.
[136] "Heritable Jurisdictions (Scotland) Act 1746," UK Legislation.
[137] See Pittock, *Culloden*, p. 102.

Figure 22 "The Execution of the Earl of Kilmarnock and Lord Balmerino." National Library of Scotland. Creative Commons 4.0.

form about the capture, movement and trials of prisoners, pamphlets and other longer printed works turned this information into a longer narrative arc that emphasized the executions as a purging of the body politic.[138] Works such as *A Narrative of the Whole Proceedings of Court at St. Margaret's Hill, Southwark* and *A Genuine Account of the Behaviour, Confession, and Dying Words, of Francis Townly [sic], (Nominal) Colonel of the Manchester Regiment, Thomas Deacon, James Dawson, John Barwick, George Fletcher and Andrew Blood, Captains in the Manchester Regiment* asserted the justice of the punishments meted out to the prisoners. Printed works discussing the Jacobite peers were especially popular, with accounts of their lives, their reasons for joining the Jacobite cause, their capture and, in the case of Kilmarnock, Balmerino and Lovat, their behavior on the scaffold being published in multiple editions at different price points, ranging from cheap pamphlets to longer and more expensive versions with copperplate engravings of each of the peers.[139]

As in 1716, popular histories of the rising also shaped events. *A Compleat and Authentick History of the Rise, Progress and Extinction of the Late Rebellion*, for example, minimizes the danger that the Jacobites had posed to the British state, asserting that "the Rebellion was certainly alarming, though not terrible."[140] Along with other works like *The History of the Rebellion Raised Against His Majesty King George II From its Rise in August 1745, to Its Happy Extinction* and Andrew Henderson's *A History of the Rebellion, 1745 and 1746*, *A Compleat and Authentick History* creates a sense of the inevitability of the defeat of the Jacobites by presenting the rising as a story with a beginning, a middle and an ending.[141]

There were also chapbooks published as part of the anti-Jacobite media explosion in 1746. As Anette Hagan explains, chapbooks are "little unbound pamphlets consisting usually of eight, twelve, sixteen or twenty-four and occasionally forty-eight pages, printed on both sides of a single folio sheet or half sheet of cheap paper and usually adorned with an often crude woodcut on the title page."[142] The first chapbook to address the 1745 rising, *The Battle of Drummossie-Muir*, was printed shortly after the Battle of Culloden and contained *Three Excellent New Songs*: "The Battle of Drummossie-Muir near Inverness, April 16th 1746," "The True Briton's Love to King George, and Rejoicing at the Victory" and "An Address to the Rebels." These served both

---

[138] See, for example, *A Genuine Account* and *A Narrative*.

[139] See, for example, *Trials of William Earl of Kilmarnock* and Wilkinson, *Trials of the Rebel Lords*.

[140] *Compleat and Authentick History*, p. 2.

[141] See *Compleat and Authentick History; History of the Rebellion*; and Henderson, *A History of the Rebellion*.

[142] Hagan, "Jacobite Chapbooks."

to disseminate news of the government's victory as well as to establish a pro-government perspective among common people. Notable among these early cheap works is the chapbook seller Dougal Graham's *A Full, Particular and True Account of the Rebellion in the Years 1745–6*. Related in the vernacular and employing rhyming octavo couplets, Graham's *Account* offered a popular poetic encapsulation of the events of the rising along with editorial anti-Jacobite commentary, as can be seen in his description of the first military encounter between the Jacobites and the Hanoverians:

> Now of their Warring I begin,
> Their cowardly Tricks as you shall fin'
> A small Party of our Soldiers clos'd in a Glen,
> Some Quarters crav'd but three were slain;
> The rest in Prison have they cast,
> With Hunger and Cold they keep them fast.
> Then *Inversnade* took by a Wyle,
> By Treachery entered *Glengyle*.[143]

The fact that Graham dedicated his *Account* to "All that *read* or *hear* this Book" suggests that he was targeting a non-literate audience as well.

While the increased enforcement of laws of treason and sedition during this period meant that the vast majority of the printed works in circulation after Culloden represented a pro-government perspective, there were nevertheless also printed works which did not condemn the Jacobites. Although not a Jacobite himself, the Scottish surgeon-turned-author Tobias Smollett presented a sympathetic perspective on the defeated Jacobites in his poem, *The Tears of Scotland*, published as a pamphlet in 1746.[144] Smollett composed the work as a poetic response to the reports he heard while resident in London regarding the actions of the government troops after Culloden. Addressed to a feminized figure of the Scottish nation, Caledonia, *The Tears of Scotland* entreats her to "mourn" both the slaughter of her people as well as the destruction of her "tow'ring Spirit." Disparaging the "civil Rage and Rancour" that produced the conflict, the narrator recounts the war crimes committed against people and property in Scotland in the aftermath, pledging to bear witness to the atrocities while he remains alive:

> While the warm Blood bedews my Veins,
> And unimpair'd Remembrance reigns,
> Resentment of my Country's Fate,
> Within my filial Breast shall beat.[145]

---

[143] Rorke, *Full, Particular and True Account*, p. 6.   [144] Smollett, *Tears of Scotland*, p. 4.
[145] Smollett, *Tears of Scotland*, p. 4.

Although Smollett's poem was intended to generate sympathy for the plight of the defeated Jacobites among the general public who did not support the Stuart cause, it also undoubtedly also resonated with Jacobite readers.

Printed works published following the 1745 rising that were more strongly pro-Jacobite disguised their allegiances. *Alexis; Or, the Young Adventurer. A Novel*, for example (attributed to the Gaelic poet and Jacobite captain Alasdair Mac Mhaighstir Alasdair) presents a coded history of the recent conflict. The titular character is "a shepherd of the first rank" who seeks to remedy the "degeneracy and miseries of the lower shepherds" in his country of Robustia (Scotland) as well as to address the situation of the neighboring nation of Felicia (England) who are in a "dire and grovelling state."[146] A fierce battle on the "unlucky plain of Lachrymania" follows, and the Felicians' leader, Sanguinarius, "rides triumphant in gore" directing scenes of *"Shocking barbarity"* in the aftermath.[147] Like Charles Edward Stuart, Alexis escapes with the help of loyal followers, including Heroica, a fictional equivalent of Flora MacDonald, who disguises Alexis as her maid. Alexis himself articulates a message designed to reassure followers of the Jacobites. Despite the dismal outcome of the rising, he remains convinced that he is "under the peculiar care of heaven" and that he will ultimately be triumphant: "All is well, and will *yet* be better."[148] Despite its not so subtle Jacobite overtones, *Alexis* was popular, even influencing other narratives focused on the escape of Charles Edward Stuart such as *Ascanius, or the Young Adventurer* (1746), *The Wanderer: or Surprising Escape* (1747) and *Young Juba: Being the History of the Young Chevalier* (1748).

2.6 Othering Jacobites after 1745

In the process of shaping the memories of 1745, the works examined in this section also mapped out a spatial and temporal account of the British nation as a site of modernity. The printed works produced after the 1715 rising largely focused on containing and minimizing the conflicts that broke out around Britain, blaming their occurrence for the most part on Catholic (and Episcopalian) religious interests or on the machinations of the French government. In the aftermath of the 1745 rising, however, while these issues were still present, commentators demonstrated much more concern with considering how social circumstances could explain the reasons why so many subjects chose to rise against the established government. As support for the Jacobite cause was more concentrated in Scotland during the 1745 rising, especially in the Highlands, Scottish and Highland culture in particular were suspect. The clan

---

[146] *Alexis*, p. 3; p. 4.　　[147] *Alexis*, p. 5.　　[148] *Alexis*, p. 6; p. 10.

system, for example, was perceived as encouraging slavish devotion to a clan chief instead of loyalty to the Crown.

Accounts of the trials and executions published after the suppression of the rising, as well as providing commentary on the biographical particulars of each prisoner, also discuss the general cultural milieu which encouraged individuals to rebel against the established government. The author of *Memoirs of the Life of Lord Lovat* uses the history of the Fraser clan to reflect on the "present situation," for example, observing that the members of current Fraser clan followed "the example of one man" who they were led by "prejudice and fatal blindness" to believe was their "sovereign and head."[149] *The Life, Adventures, and Many and Great Vicissitudes of Fortune of SIMON, Lord LOVAT* expands these comments to apply to all Highland troops: "We are now truly inform'd of the Strength, Prowess, and Capacity of those brutish savages who inhabit the Highlands of Scotland, their Manner of Life, their blind Dependence upon, and passive Subjection to their Lairds and Sovereign Proprietors."[150]

The popular histories of the '45 also devote considerable attention to representing Highland otherness. In his *History of the Present Rebellion,* John Marchant repeats passages from the sixteenth-century Scottish historian George Buchanan in order to give a "Character" of the Highlanders,[151] as does the author of *A Journey Through Part of England and Scotland, Along with the Army Under the Command of His Royal Highness the Duke of Cumberland* in his description of "the *Manners* and *Customs* of the different People, especially of the *Highlanders*"; the latter, however, notes that he includes "some Alteration, it being very applicable to the present Time."[152] The uncouth behavior of the Highlanders is in turn used to explain their propensity to rebel. As Marchant asserts, "the Highlanders, in all Reigns, have been remarkable for disturbing the established Government of *Scotland,* by taking up Arms of every Invasion for the Invaders, and have been the Ringleaders and chief Promoters of the Rebellion."[153] Graham's vivid descriptions of the Jacobite army in *A Full, Particular and True Account of the Rebellion in the Years 1745–6* also reinforces the image of Highlanders as rapacious barbarians:

> Of Skin and Wood, a Targe on their Arms,
> Stuck full of Nails, for stenting Harms;
> Wanting the Breeks, light for to rin,
> Their Thighs made red with Weet and Win';
> Some barefoot for lack of Blogs [shoes],
> Riven [torn] Hips with Hether and Scrogs [brushwood].[154]

---

[149] *Memoirs of the Life of Lord Lovat,* p. 11.

[150] *Life, Adventures, and Many and Great Vicissitudes,* p. v.   [151] Marchant, *History,* p. 18.

[152] *A Journey,* p. 175.   [153] Marchant, *History,* p. 18.

[154] Rorke, *Full, Particular and True Account,* p. 93.

The discourse circulating in popular narratives in the post-Culloden era encouraged the development of a stadial theory of culture as Scottish writers and thinkers attempted to find ways of explaining the rising by suggesting the fundamental otherness of the Highlands was due to its existing at an earlier stage of civilization than the rest of Britain.

2.7 Knotted Memories of the 1745 Rising

As indicated previously, the 1745 rising took place at a historical juncture during which the print marketplace were expanding rapidly. Competition for readers was paramount, and printers in urban centers in England, Scotland and Ireland (as well as in the American colonies) were eager to sell their products to a reading population who were hungry for the latest news and entertainment about current events, especially events that had been so consequential for the nation. The periodical *The Parrot*, attributed to Eliza Haywood, comments on the inordinate focus on the mediation of events post-Culloden: "all the Conversation I have heard for I know not how long, has been wholly on Indictments, – Trials – Sentences of Death, and Executions … how do some People dwell upon it!"[155] In such a competitive market situation, novelty was imperative. Printers consequently capitalized on all opportunities to edge out the competition by producing new editions that included additional materials that they promised would provide readers with deeper insight, a more comprehensive perspective or more salacious details. The growth of the marketplace and competition of the market system also provided the circumstances for more knots of memory, including the articulation of counter-memories even within works supporting the official government position. In an attempt to be as comprehensive as possible, to capture the interest of new readers or to entice readers edition to purchase a new edition of a work which they had already purchased, later editions of previously printed works often included substantially more material representing the Jacobite perspective than the earlier editions.

A second edition of *A Narrative of the Whole Proceedings of Court at St. Margaret's Hill, Southwark*, for example, with the title slightly altered to *An Authentick Narrative of the Whole Proceedings of Court at St. Margaret's Hill, Southwark*, included not only the trials against the Manchester Regiment, as appeared in the original, but also the "Trials of the *Scots* Rebels" and, most notably, the "Dying Speeches" of the nine Jacobites executed at Kennington Common. As we have seen, execution speeches and other materials were eagerly consumed by adherents as well as detractors of the Jacobites. Despite expressing disapproval of the fact that "the very last Action" of the Scottish Jacobite prisoners "was to scatter and disperse Papers among the Multitude"

---

[155] Haywood, *The Parrot*, p. 4.

that were "full of Treason," *An Authentick Narrative* reproduces those very speeches.[156] In a similar fashion, the second edition of Henderson's *A History of the Rebellion, 1745 and 1746* supplemented its historical narrative with "All the DECLARATIONS of the PRETENDER, and the JOURNAL of his Marches through *ENGLAND*, as published by himself,"[157] giving a retrospective voice to those whom the government wished to silence. The popular printed material circulating after Culloden therefore constitutes "knots of memories" that, even as they assert their loyalty to the Hanoverian regime, inadvertently also reproduce the perspectives of those who rose against the government. At the same time as these narratives served to marginalize the peripheries of the British archipelago, they also inscribed some of the counter-memories of the margins – however attenuated – into the stored printed memories of the nation.

Accounts of the '45, trials of the rebels and the rebel lords, narratives concerning the escape of Charles Stuart and chapbooks concerning Jacobites continued to be printed and reprinted in locations including London, Edinburgh, Dublin, Boston and Philadelphia from 1746 steadily up to the mid-nineteenth century along with other popular print items such as engravings and maps. Beginning in the late eighteenth century, however, new representations began to appear in popular and literary works, revising and reshaping the memory of the Jacobites and the Jacobite cause for a new age.

3 Re-membering Jacobitism, 1747–1830

In this section, I shift from focusing on the representations of Jacobitism during the active military campaigns and diplomatic endeavors during first half of the eighteenth century to examining the remembering of the Jacobite movement in the later eighteenth and the early nineteenth centuries. Scholars have noted how, over the course of roughly eighty years, Jacobites changed from being considered criminals and traitors to the British crown to being remembered as representatives of a pre-industrial culture renowned for their hardiness and loyalty as well as sentimental figures of a lost, but cherished, Scottish nationhood.[158] Here I investigate the ways in which these changes were effected through a complex process of multi-mediation as I consider how, during this time, literary works in oral, manuscript and print media served, in Ann Rigney's terms, to relay and recalibrate the cultural memory of the Jacobites.[159] I pay particular attention to the counter-memories articulated in Jacobite sources, including Irish Gaelic and Scots Gaelic sources, noting how traces of these traditions migrated into the wider English-language

---

[156] *An Authentick Narrative*, p. iv.   [157] Henderson, *Edinburgh History*.

[158] See especially Pittock, *Culloden* and *Poetry and Jacobite Politics*; Kidd, "Rehabilitation"; and Womack, *Improvement*.

[159] Rigney, "Dynamics," 356.

print marketplace. While I briefly take into account well-known literary texts that have been treated extensively by other critics (the songs of Robert Burns and the novels of Walter Scott, for example), I also analyze genres and texts that have not been fully considered in other studies of Jacobitism to date, including manuscript works and chapbooks. Rigney comments on the shifting nature of culture memory: "As the performative aspect of the term 'remembrance' suggests, collective memory is constantly 'in the works' and, like a swimmer, has to keep moving even just to stay afloat."[160] Drawing from Rigney's and Erll's theories on the construction and afterlife of cultural memories, this section investigates how both literary and popular works helped store the Jacobite memories created in the earlier era, re-shaping them and keeping them in the public eye and consciousness. My point is that, rather than just being assimilated into a homogeneous dominant cultural memory after the threat of Jacobitism was over, Jacobite counter-memories remained fluid, capable of being re-activated to fit multiple, sometimes conflicting, political uses in the century following Culloden.

3.1 Re-collecting the Jacobites: "The Lyon in Mourning" Manuscript of Robert Forbes

I begin by considering one of the most important mediations of Jacobite cultural memory by the Jacobites themselves in the years after the 1745 rising, "The Lyon in Mourning" manuscript compiled by the Episcopalian minister Robert Forbes between 1747 and 1775. "The Lyon in Mourning" includes not just accounts by and about well-known historical figures, but also the stories and perspectives of ordinary men and women who were involved in the Jacobite cause during the 1745 rising. Forbes himself spent the majority of the time of the rising in prison, as he was arrested in early September 1745 on his way to join the forces of Charles Edward Stuart. He was released in May 1746, and, in the midst of the government suppression and persecution of Jacobites, he turned his attention to recording the experiences of his fellow insurgents, collecting whatever manuscript materials that he could find as well as organizing interviews with eye-witnesses whose words he transcribed. Forbes's chief concern in creating and curating his extensive manuscript was to preserve the materials that represented the experiences of Jacobites. As he writes, "I have a great Anxiety to make the Collection as compleat & exact as possible for the Instruction of future Ages in a piece of History the most remarkable & interesting that ever happened in any Age or Country."[161] His comments suggest his acute understanding of the processes of selective memory and cultural

---

[160] Rigney, "Dynamics," 345.
[161] Forbes, "Lyon," 4: 787. References indicating volume and page number are from the digitised copy available at Simon Fraser University Library: https://dhil.lib.sfu.ca/lyoninmourning/.

amnesia that would be used to shape recent events, as, in a letter to his correspondent Major MacDonald of Glenaladale, he notes, "one can never be too strict and nice, especially in an Age when even glaring Facts are most impudently denied and contradicted with the greatest Boldness."[162] Forbes scribed enough material to fill ten octavo volumes between 1747 and the year of his death (1775), each with a title page including the date of composition, a Latin epigraph and the title (see Figure 23).

Forbes exercised great caution in preserving his materials. The subtitle of the work identifies its contents, but leaves the reference to Charles Edward Stuart blank: "A Collection (as exactly made as the Iniquity of the Times would permit) of Speeches, Letters, Journals, &c. relative to the Affairs, but more particularly, the Dangers & Distresses of . . ."[163] Forbes's choice to avoid using the name of the Stuart heir on the cover is odd, however, because even a cursory glance at a few of the many items contained in the volumes would be enough to confirm their treasonous nature. There are speeches from the scaffold by a number of the Jacobite prisoners who were executed, including two versions of the speech by Lord Balmerino (one of which is identified as "faithfully transcribed from his Lordship's own Hand-writ").[164] There are narrative accounts of atrocities, including, for example, information provided by Mrs. Cameron, Dr. Archibald Cameron's wife, about the plundering and indignities carried out by government soldiers after Culloden.[165] Forbes also included copies of many letters to and from his correspondents in a network that ranged from Bath to Benbecula. In addition, he took pains to interview as many individuals as possible who played a part in Charles Edward Stuart's flight through the Highlands and Islands. He includes, for instance, the "journals" of the soldier and Gaelic poet Alasdair MacMhaistir Alasdair/Alexander MacDonald; the narrative of the Gaelic-speaking sedan chairman, Ned Burke (or Bourke), who served as personal servant to Charles Edward Stuart; and details from a conversation with Flora MacDonald, who disguised Charles Edward Stuart as her maidservant Betty Burke to facilitate his escape. The manuscript also features a number of poems, including, for instance, a poem in Latin by Donald Roy MacDonald "concerning the want of the Highland Dress";[166] a lament after the defeat at the Battle of Culloden "said to have been completed by a Scots Gentleman, an Officer in the Dutch service";[167] a satire addressed "To Mr Secretary Murray, on his turning Evidence, by the Revd Mr Thomas Drummond, Edr, 1747";[168] and sentimental verses "Upon a Young Lady, who died on seeing her Lover, Mr Dawson, executed on the 30th of July, 1746."[169] In the latter,

---

[162] Forbes, "Lyon," 7: 1496.   [163] Forbes, "Lyon," title page of volume 1.
[164] Forbes, "Lyon," 1: 108.   [165] Forbes, "Lyon," 3: 347–57.   [166] Forbes, "Lyon," 8: 1622.
[167] Forbes, "Lyon," 3: 389–91.   [168] Forbes, "Lyon," 3: 411–13.
[169] Forbes, "Lyon," 3: 407.

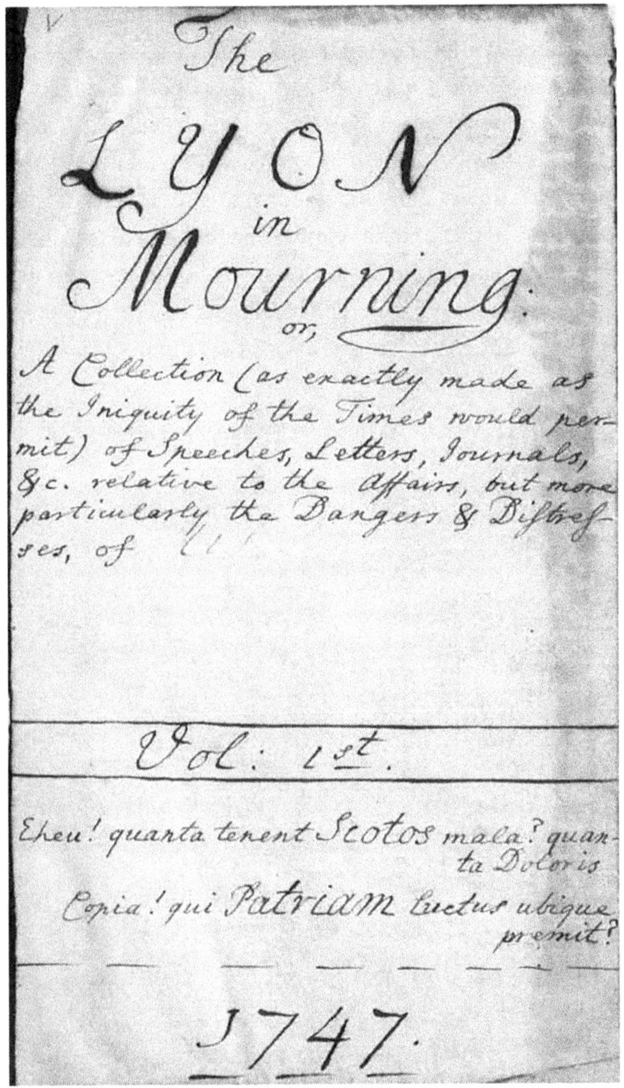

Figure 23 "The Lyon in Mourning" Title page, Vol. 1. Simon Fraser University Digitized Collections. https://dhil.lib.sfu.ca/lyoninmourning/ Open Access.

Dawson's beloved expires upon seeing the cruelties inflicted on his body, only, it is suggested, to be reunited with him in Heaven:

> At once she burst ye feeble Bonds of Clay;
> And her free Soul, exulting, springs away.
> To endless Bliss they issue out of Pain.
> One Moment separates, & joins again.[170]

---

[170] Forbes, "Lyon," 3: 407.

In addition to manuscript items, "The Lyon in Mourning" also contains two printed works bound within the volumes. Volume 1 contains *The Communion Office For the Use of the Church of Scotland* which belonged to Reverend Robert Lyon, a Jacobite executed after Culloden; and volume 5 includes a copy of *Alexis; or, The Young Adventurer, A Novel*. In addition, material items associated with the Stuart heir are fixed onto the covers of several of the volumes, including a piece of a garter that belonged to Charles Edward Stuart, apron strings and fabric from the gown he wore when in disguise as Betty Burke and fragments of the eight-oared boat in which he traveled around the islands while evading government troops (see Figure 24).

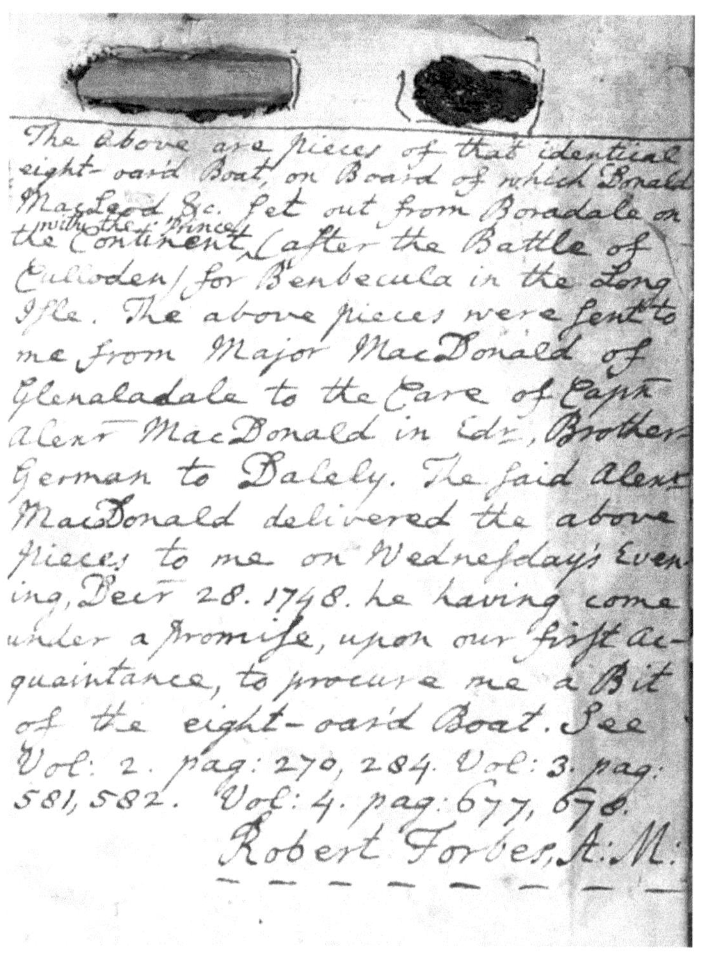

Figure 24 "The Lyon in Mourning," Volume 4 back boards. Simon Fraser University Digitized Collections. https://dhil.lib.sfu.ca/lyoninmourning/ Open Access.

"The Lyon in Mourning" was never published during Forbes's lifetime, but it eventually became the property of the historian, author and journalist Robert Chambers. In 1834, Chambers published sections of the manuscript in *Jacobite Memoirs of the Rebellion of 1745* and also drew on the manuscript in his revised *History of the Rebellion of 1745–6* in 1840.[171] He subsequently bequeathed "The Lyon in Mourning" to the Faculty of Advocates, and after his death in 1871, the manuscript became the property of the Advocates Library which became the National Library of Scotland in 1925. A three-volume printed edition was produced by the Scottish History Society in 1895–1896, but, although it made the contents of the manuscript available to a wider audience, the printed edition also fundamentally changed the work, representing it as an edited collection of accounts rather than a work of cultural and personal memory. The manuscript is currently the focus of a digital humanities partnership project between the National Library of Scotland and Simon Fraser University's Research Centre for Scottish Studies and Digital Humanities Innovation Lab who are analyzing the manuscript with particular attention to references to women, Gaelic-speakers and laboring-class individuals in the manuscript.

3.2 1745 in the Irish and Scottish Gaelic Traditions

In Gaelic-speaking Ireland, as Vincent Morley observes, "The 1745 rising prompted a flood of Jacobite compositions," many of which focused more on the threat that the Jacobites posed to the Hanoverian government when they "advanced into the heart of England" rather than their eventual defeat.[172] Irish Gaelic Jacobite verse was being democratized during this time, with poems being "written in accentual metres suitable for singing." As Morley suggests, "by the 1740s, such lyrics were commonly set to popular airs," some of which "have secured permanent places in the Irish song tradition."[173] The content of Irish Gaelic Jacobite verse was also shifting away from "the restoration of the pre-1691 ancien régime" toward resistance to the ruling establishment.[174]

In Scotland, as in Ireland, the 1745 produced a profusion of responses from Gaelic-language poets. As in the Irish Gaelic tradition, a number of the Scots Gaelic Jacobite tunes and songs from this time and earlier found their way into collections in the later eighteenth century such as David Herd's *Ancient and Modern Scottish Songs, Heroic Ballads* (1776) and Joseph Ritson's *Scotish [sic] Songs* (1794). But there were important differences between the Irish Gaelic and Scottish Gaelic Jacobite cultural productions. As the geographical site for much of the 1745 conflict, Scotland was immediately impacted by events during the rising,

---

[171] Chambers, *Jacobite Memoirs*; *Select Writings*.   [172] Morley, "Irish Jacobitism," p. 37.
[173] Morley, "Irish Jacobitism," p. 37.   [174] Morley, "Irish Jacobitism," p. 37.

and its Stuart-supporting inhabitants suffered accordingly during the suppression
and aftermath. As indicated in the previous section, the Highland Scots were also
subjected to forms of colonial knowledge-production that cast them as primitive
others to the civilized anglicized self. Domhnall Uilleam Stiùbhart observes that
Gaelic poetry of the 1745 "offers us a plethora of different voices and perspectives
on its events: optimism and calls to action during the campaign; bitterness and
disorientation after Culloden; threats of bloodthirsty revenge following
British atrocities throughout the region; modulating into later efforts to
rally a united Gaelic front to avenge the humiliation of the heavy-handed
Act of Proscription."[175] Such representations of Jacobite cultural memory
indicate the divided perspectives that existed within the Scottish Gaelic
communities in the aftermath of Culloden.

Unlike in Ireland, the aftermath of the 1745 saw a burgeoning of Scots Gaelic
print culture, reflecting an effort to assimilate and improve the "primitive"
Highlands by educating its population to read and write. Stiùbhart discusses the
impact of the shift to printing Gaelic that occurred in the half-century after
Culloden: "From the mid-eighteenth century onwards, systematic endeavours to
codify and refine a 'pure' written standard of Scottish Gaelic were complemented
by initiatives to record and evaluate poetry, songs, and proverbs, some of which
were subsequently disseminated in printed anthologies."[176] As Stiùbhart indicates,
projects such as the translation of the New Testament into Scots Gaelic, the
production of a Scots Gaelic Dictionary and the compilation of an anthology of
Scots Gaelic poetry anthology were designed to represent Scots Gaelic as
a language of Enlightenment.

In the case of the first printed book of secular Scots Gaelic poetry, *Ais-eiridh na
Sean Chànoin Albannaich* [*The Resurrection of the Ancient Scottish Language*]
(1751) by Alasdair mac Mhaighstir Alasdair/Alexander MacDonald, however, the
encouragement for printing and regularizing the Scots Gaelic language went hand
in hand with the continued expression of Jacobite sentiments. Mac Mhaighstir
Alasdair had served in Clanranald's Regiment in the Jacobite army during the '45
and was also one of Forbes's informants. In the Preface to *Ais-eiridh na Sean
Chànoin Albannaich*, written in English, he indicates his purpose: to provide
a published version of poems "wrote some time ago, for the amusement of
a private gentleman" for the entertainment and edification of those who could
read Gaelic; and to raise in those readers who did not speak Gaelic a desire to learn
the language so that they could appreciate "the charms of poetry and rhetoric" that
it contains.[177] Moreover, he voices a hope that his work will also encourage better

---

[175] Stiùbhart, "Adaptation," p. 37.   [176] Stiùbhart, "Gaelic Enlightenment," p. 149.
[177] Mac Mhaighstir Alasdair, *Ais-eiridh*, p. v.

understanding of the "genius" of the Scots Gaelic language, which he claims is a contemporary remnant of the once-powerful "CELTIC nation," resulting in a new attitude toward the Highland people who are "now relegated to an obscure, neglected corner" of the world.[178] Mac Mhaighstir Alasdair voices his astonishment that "in an age in which the study of antiquity is so much in fashion" and in which "freedom of thought, love of knowledge, and moderation" are promoted, "this people and this language should be alone persecuted and intolerated."[179] At the same time, a number of the poems in *Ais-eiridh na Sean Chánoin Albannaich* voice strong pro-Stuart sentiments that are anything but moderate themselves. "Oran a rinneadh a bhliadhna 1746" ["A Song Composed in the Year 1746"], for example, praises "a' bhliadhna chorr" ["the wonderful year"] in which the king will arrive with French support, snow and frost will be banished, and joy will replace pain when the Stuart king arrives. Although the poem was ostensibly written in anticipation of the 1745 rising, its final message is still relevant in the year of the book's publication as it ends with a plea to God to cleanse Whitehall of the Hanoverians: "Relieve us of our swinish yoke,/And send the speckled, mangy brood/Of snouted hogs o'erseas" ["Tog dhinn a' mhuc 's a cuing,/'S a h-al breac, brothach, uirceineach,/Le'n cuid chrom-shoc, thar tuinn"].[180] Unlike some other printed "knots of memory," *Ais-eiridh na Sean Chánoin Albannaich* hides its Jacobite affiliations in plain sight, albeit only for those who can read the Gaelic. Mac Mhaighstir Alasdair's "Birlinn Chlann Ragnaill/Clan Ranald's Galley," written after the publication of *Ais-eiridh* and not published until 1776, also voices the poet's pro-Jacobite perspectives as it celebrates the strength and determination of the Clan Ranald sailors who work skillfully together to steer their ship through a raging storm in order to arrive safely at Carrickfergus in Ireland. The poem metaphorically celebrates the resilience of the clan in the aftermath of Culloden, reminds them of their intra-national connections and, obliquely, urges them to prepare for another potential battle and restoration.[181]

Not all of the Highland clans were Jacobite, however, and it is important to recognize that Scots Gaelic poetry was also produced by poets on the Hanoverian side. Donnchadh Bàn Mac an t-Saoir/Duncan Ban Macintyre (1724–1812), for example, who served in the Duke of Argyll's army, included works praising the government such as "Oran Do'n Righ/Song to the King" in his *Orain Ghaidhealach/Highland Songs* [1768].[182] Although he occupied a political

---

[178] Mac Mhaighstir Alasdair, *Ais-eiridh*, p. vi.

[179] Mac Mhaighstir Alasdair, *Ais-eiridh*, p. viii.

[180] Translated from Campbell, *Highland Songs*, p. 105.

[181] See Black, "Alasdair mac Mhaighstir Alasdair," p. 119; and Thomson, *Introduction*, pp. 172–80.

[182] Calder, *Gaelic Songs*. For a fuller sense of the spectrum of eighteenth-century Gaelic poetry, see Black, *An Lasair*.

position opposite to that of Mac Mhaighstir Alasdair, however, Mac an t-Saoir shared his countryman's concern for the Gaelic language and culture, later writing poems for the Highland Society in praise of Gaelic and of the bagpipes.

3.4 Reviving and Revising the "Genius of the Highlanders": James Macpherson's Ossianic Poems and Highland Tourism

A significant change in attitudes toward Jacobitism in Lowland Scotland and England occurred due to the deployment of Highland troops by the British government during the Seven Years' War (1756–1763).[183] This image of the martial Highlander was reflected and refracted in the *Poems of Ossian* by the Highland poet James Macpherson/Seumas MacMhuirich. Macpherson voices concerns like those of Mac Mhaighstir Alasdair about the negative representation of the Scottish Gaels in British culture. In *Fragments of Ancient Poetry* (1760), *Fingal: An Ancient Epic Poem in Six Books* (1762) and *Temora: An Ancient Epic Poem in Eight Books* (1763), however, he focuses attention not on the current Highland troops but on those of the past, whom he identified as the ancient Caledonians. Claiming that his works were translations of the work of a third-century Gaelic warrior-bard, Ossian, he suggests in his "A Dissertation on the Antiquity &c. of the Poems of Ossian the Son of Fingal" that part of his purpose was to address the post-1745 attitudes toward the Highlanders in the present:

> The genius of the highlanders has suffered a great change within these few years. . . . Many have now learned to leave their mountains, and seek their fortunes in a milder climate; and though a certain *amor patriae* may some-times bring them back, they have, during their absence, imbibed enough of foreign manners to despise the customs of their ancestors.[184]

Macpherson's treatment of the Highlanders is inherently ambiguous, however. On the one hand, he represents the Caledonians as mythic warriors of the past who pose no threat in the present. The narrator, Ossian, who refers to himself as the last of his race, is a blind old man who reflects nostalgically on the days when Fingal and the Caledonian heroes vanquished their enemies: "The fame of my former actions is ceased; and I sit forlorn at the tombs of my friends."[185] On the other hand, the poems of Ossian also suggest the continuing power of the past through storytelling and poetry. The characters themselves in the poems are motivated through hearing "the deeds of other times."[186] In "Fingal," the hero Fingal remarks to the Scandinavian leader, Swaran, whom he has just

---

[183] See Clyde, *From Rebel to Hero*; Mackillop, *More Fruitful*; and Devine, *Clanship*.

[184] Macpherson, *Fingal*, p. 84. Also see Ossian Online, produced by the National University of Ireland, Galway, for eighteenth-century facsimiles indicating Macpherson's use of typography and white space.

[185] Macpherson, *Fingal*, p. xv.   [186] Macpherson, *Fingal*, p. 16.

conquered, on the way that "song" outlasts both the material body and the landscape: "We shall pass away like a dream. . . . Our tombs will be lost in the heath. . . . Our names may be heard in the song, but the strength of our arms will cease."[187] The immense popularity of Macpherson's work had a positive impact on the perception of Highlanders and, by extension, Jacobites, in the late eighteenth century. As the century wore on, pressure by members of the newly formed Highland societies in London (1778) and Edinburgh (1784) resulted in the lifting of some of the official prohibitions against the Highlanders. The Highland Dress Act was repealed in 1782, and a parliamentary bill for the restoration of the Forfeited Estates was passed in 1784.

The Poems of Ossian also influenced other writers on the periphery of Britain, inspiring writers such as Evan Evans (*Some Specimens of the Poetry of Antient Welsh Bards* [1764]) and Iolo Morganwg (*Barddoniaeth Dafydd ab Gwilym* [1789] and *The Myvyrian Archaiology of Wales* [1801 and 1807]) in Wales and Joseph Cooper Walker (*Historical Memoirs of the Irish Bards* [1786]) and Charlotte Brooke (*Reliques of Irish Poetry* [1789]) in Ireland to explore the "ancient" bardic poetry of their own locations as a marker of national identities, as well as prompting the English Bishop Thomas Percy to develop his ideas of the Teutonic minstrel origins of English balladry in opposition to claims for bardic nationalism.[188]

In addition, the popularity of Macpherson's Caledonian heroes fed a growing interest in travel and tourism to the Scottish Highlands, in tandem with a vogue for the sublime as articulated in works such as Edmund Burke's *A Philosophical Enquiry into the Origin of the Sublime and the Beautiful* (1757). As Nigel Leask comments, "the popularity of the *Poems of Ossian* in the early 1760s remapped Highland topography"; it stimulated "enthusiasm for Gaelic culture which ironically coincided with official attempts to extirpate the language" and "provided a new incentive for tourists to visit the Highlands."[189] Tourists to the Highlands in the late eighteenth century such as Thomas Pennant (*Tour in Scotland 1769* [1771] and *Tour in Scotland and Voyage to the Hebrides 1772* [1771–76]), Samuel Johnson (*A Journey to the Western Islands of Scotland* [1775]) and James Boswell (*The Journal of a Tour to the Hebrides* [1785]) helped generate a sentimental attitude to Jacobitism as an exotic but extinct feature of British history and geopolitics (despite the furor over Johnson's attitude to Scotland).[190] Boswell's *Journal* even featured a section entitled an "Authentic Account of the

---

[187] Macpherson, *Fingal*, p. 79.   [188] See Trumpener, *Bardic Nationalism*.

[189] Leask, *Stepping Westward*, p. 19.

[190] See Rogers, *Johnson and Boswell*. The Curious Travellers 2 project, headed by Mary-Ann Constantine and Nigel Leask, is currently producing open-access digital editions of Pennant's Tours of Wales and Scotland.

Distresses and Escape of the Grandson of King James II in the Year 1746" that echoed the pro-Jacobite accounts of Charles Edward Stuart's escape.[191] The visits to the Highlands by later literary tourists such as Dorothy and William Wordsworth and John Keats ensured that sentimental Jacobitism would feature within the canon of English Romantic-era poetry.

3.5 Re-purposing the Politics of Jacobitism in English Poetry: Thomas Campbell and Anne Grant

The cultural rehabilitation of Jacobites in Britain was shaped in new ways in the wake of the revolutions in America, France and Haiti, the Irish Rebellion, and the wars into which Britain was plunged in the late eighteenth century. But the change of attitude toward the Jacobites was complicated as it also potentially involved criticism of the British government in the past and, by extension, in the present. "Lochiel's Warning," by the Lowland Scottish poet Thomas Campbell, for example, represents a positive perspective on Jacobitism, while also registering a critique of the government suppression of democratic reform.

Born in Glasgow, Campbell spent summers in Argyllshire working as a tutor while he attended university. His biographer speculates that it was during his perambulations in this area that he conceived of the idea of "Lochiel's Warning." Campbell's reading of John Home's *History of the Rebellion in the Year 1745* (1802) also seems to have been influential, as he quoted that work in an early draft of his poem.[192] "Lochiel's Warning," published originally in 1803 and included in the 1803 and subsequent editions of Campbell's enormously popular *The Pleasures of Hope, With Other Poems,* unfolds as a dialogue between a Wizard "seer" and Donald Cameron of Lochiel, chief of clan Cameron and an influential supporter of Charles Edward Stuart's campaign. Accosting Lochiel before the final military conflict at Culloden, the Wizard predicts disaster for the Jacobite forces during the battle:

> Lochiel! Lochiel! Beware of the day
> When the Lowlands shall meet thee in battle array!
> For a field of the dead rushes red on my sight,
> And the clans of Culloden are scattered in fight.[193]

Moving beyond the carnage on the field to describe the burning of Lochiel's house, the Wizard also foresees the destruction wrought upon the Highland lands and people by the government troops:

> For the blackness of ashes shall mark where it stood,
> And a wild mother scream o'er her famishing brood.[194]

---

[191] Boswell, *Journal*, pp. 215–40.   [192] Beattie, *Life*, pp. 1, 177; see Davis, "Rehabilitating."
[193] Campbell, *Pleasures*, p. 107.   [194] Campbell, *Pleasures*, p. 109.

The Wizard's prophecy does not deter Lochiel, however, who gallantly asserts the bravery of the Jacobite forces: "Their swords are a thousand, their bosoms are one!/They are true to the land of their blood and their breath."[195] When the Wizard presses his point further, indicating the probable fate of those who will survive the battlefield – exile or execution – Lochiel announces his own intention to leave "no blot on his name" through any of his actions, but rather to "Look proudly to heaven from the death-bed of fame."[196] Campbell's poem remakes the figure of the Jacobite into a heroic, albeit tragic figure. But in his graphic description of Cumberland and his troops "insulting the slain" and "blast[ing] and burn[ing]" the Highlands and of the tortured death of the condemned Jacobite prisoner, Campbell also presents a negative image of the systemic violence of the British monarchy and government, an image that also resonated in Campbell's own era of government repressions against those advocating democratic reform.[197] In "Lochiel's Warning," Lochiel and his clansmen are recalibrated as Campbell shifts the emphasis from the Jacobites' support of the divine right of kings to their support of each other as they face violence at the hands of their government.

The year 1803 also saw another poetic recalibration of the Jacobites: Anne Grant's epic poetic narrative, "The Highlanders," first published in *Poems on Various Subjects*. Like Campbell, Grant focuses attention on Highland clan society, but while Campbell presents a retrospective view that emphasizes the past military prowess of the clans, Grant's poem is set in the present and focuses on the negative effects of the aftermath of the 1745, including the loss of traditional social bonds and the depopulation of the Highlands. Grant celebrates the traditional communitarianism of the Highland clans, but suggests that their way of life has now been destroyed. Drawing on her own experience as a resident of the Highlands, Grant's speaker indicates that the "social joys and cheerful toils" with which she was familiar are now "dead": "In vain my eyes the length'ning vale explore,/From hillocks green the blue smokes rise no more."[198] The clan chiefs have vanished, the people have dispersed, and even the bards who kept the culture alive have emigrated "across the Atlantic's roar":

> No more the bard, whom native genius fires,
> (Celestial flame, that heaven-ward still aspires),
> Bids patriot valour in full glory blaze,
> Or consecrates departed worth with praise.[199]

---

195 Campbell, *Pleasures*, p. 114.   196 Campbell, *Pleasures*, p. 116.
197 Campbell, *Pleasures*, p. 107; pp. 112–13.   198 Grant, *Poems*, pp. 23–24.
199 Grant, *Poems*, p. 25.

For Grant, these changes constitute a tragedy not just for the Highlanders who are directly impacted, but also for the health of British society which is suffering from a lack of fortitude and moral fiber. In Part I, Grant praises the hardy Highlanders in the north for their strength of body and of character. She compares them positively to the inhabitants of the south, who are enfeebled from being caught up in a world of luxury and ease. Parts II and III delineate the "local habits of the Celtic race,"[200] describing the pastoral life of the Highlanders as they adapt to the rhythms of the natural world, moving to the shielings in summer and further down the mountains in the winter. Grant's detailed descriptions of the Highland social activities are aimed in particular at reversing the negative view of the Highlanders established after 1745 as she urges those who "on soft Luxury's velvet lap reclin'd" not to judge the Highlanders as "uncouth and wild."[201] Rather, Grant holds a mirror up to her readers, suggesting that they themselves are like "sportive insects of a summer day," who are not designed to survive challenging times.[202] In the conflicts of the present-day especially, Grant implies, Britain needs what traditional Highland society can offer.

Part 3, focusing on the love story between the "Swain" Farquhar and his beloved Moraig, encourages readers to connect the changes that have occurred to Highland society to the government's actions during and after the 1745 rising. The two lovers' relationship, which developed through a chance encounter when Farquhar went searching for his missing cattle, is violently interrupted when Moraig's brothers join the Jacobite cause. Grant's representation of the destruction of Moraig's family dwelling points a finger at the mercilessness of the government troops at the time. At the conclusion of Part 4, Moraig and her family, including her defeated brothers who have returned home, are resettled into Farquhar's household, which has avoided being drawn into the conflict. In such a way, Grant provides a model of rehabilitation of Jacobites. Instead of the violence which was meted out after 1745, a violence that Grant blames for the subsequent rupture in Highland culture, she offers a representation of peaceful re-integration which preserves the existing social system.

Part 5 of "The Highlanders" focuses more directly on the aftermath of the 1745 by depicting actual historical characters and events. Grant describes the escape of Charles Edward Stuart after Culloden sympathetically. She also portrays the arrest and trial of Flora MacDonald. Whereas the trial and execution pamphlets and popular histories that circulated immediately after the 1715 and 1745 risings were concerned to dissuade readers from feeling compassion

---

[200] Grant, *Poems*, p. 31.   [201] Grant, *Poems*, p. 26.   [202] Grant, *Poems*, p. 27.

for the Jacobites, in "The Highlanders," Grant attempts to develop readerly identification with the people involved in the rising.

Part of that identification involves Grant's providing greater insight into the affordances of oral culture which integrate individuals into community in Highland culture. In "The Highlanders," Grant depicts a society which is woven together through oral music, song and story. She makes frequent comparisons between the Highland mediascape and the literary landscape in the rest of Britain which, she suggests, encourages a flawed perspective on the world. In her poem, Grant combines the simplicity and purity of oral culture with the formality and possibilities of an epic print culture format. She self-identifies as "a rustic Muse" who is concerned with presenting "the British song" to touch "the British heart" and asks readers to listen to her simple truths.[203] Grant herself translates those simple truths of oral culture into a literary landscape, however, as "The Highlanders" employs heroic couplets with frequent allusions to the monumental poem of an earlier Scottish poet, James Thomson, who also worked in heroic couplets to portray the beauties of nature as a reflection of the moral universe. In Grant's work, we see an early nineteenth-century association of Jacobitism with sentimentality. But as Pam Perkins and Juliet Shields remind us, such representations were drawing from the sentimentalism that had been a Jacobite literary trope since the late seventeenth century.[204]

Grant was a prolific writer who cultivated an extensive network of corres-pondents and supporters. As someone who lived in the Gaelic-speaking Highlands for twenty-two years and who was directly acquainted with individ-uals who had themselves been or whose relatives had been involved in the 1745 rising, she had extensive firsthand experience to draw on. Her further reflections on the subject of Jacobitism such as *Letters from the Mountains* (1806) and *Essays on the Superstitions of the Highlanders* (1811) offer a unique combination of personal knowledge and documentary evidence.[205] Grant's impact on the cultural memory of Jacobitism, however, like Campbell's, was overshadowed by the appearance of another writer who was turning to the Scottish past for literary inspiration at the beginning of the nineteenth century: Walter Scott. In considering Scott's powerful reconfiguration of the cultural memory of the Jacobites, it is crucial not to forget the impact that Campbell and, especially, Grant, had on the cultural memory of the Jacobites in the short time period before *Waverley* (1814) was published.

---

[203] Grant, *Poems*, p. 29.　　[204] Perkins, "The 'candour'" and Shields, *Sentimental Literature*.
[205] See Perkins, "Anne Grant and the Social Networks of Jacobitism."

3.6 Novel Perspectives: Walter Scott and the Aftermath of *Waverley*

Like Grant, Scott was powerfully moved by accounts that he heard in his childhood by individuals who shared their memories of the 1745 rising. He also collected books and archival material detailing Scottish history, including multiple copies of *Ascanius* as well as of other popular items published in the wake of the 1745 rising. In *The Minstrelsy of the Scottish Border*, he had achieved considerable success in anthologizing Lowland ballads and poems, while his sensationally popular narrative poems based on Scottish history such as *The Lay of the Last Minstrel* (1805), *Marmion* (1808) and *The Lady of the Lake* (1810), for example, earned him the offer of the poet laureateship (which he declined) in 1813. Around the year 1808, Scott started drafting the work that would constitute the most powerful recalibration of the 1745 in British cultural memory in the nineteenth century: *Waverley; or, Tis Sixty Years Hence*. The novel was published in 1814.

Scott's cultivation of sympathy for the Jacobites in *Waverley* was influenced by some of the same concerns that motivated Campbell and Grant. But where Campbell and Grant indicate an imaginative role for the Jacobite cause in the contemporary moment, either as revolutionary spirits or as models of loyalty and morality, Scott relegates the cultural memory of the Jacobites to the past. Although *Waverley* suggests the attractions of Jacobitism and portrays individual Jacobites such as Fergus and Flora MacIvor sympathetically, it also works to contain the memory of the Stuarts and their followers within the bounds of history.

Waverley is both a *Bildungsroman* constructed around the story of main character, Edward Waverley, as well as a stadial history of the British nation. Scott skillfully combines the two projects in order to suggest the interconnection of the individual and the imagined community of the nation. The English Edward, who signs up to fight on the government side during the 1745 rising, decides to visit an old friend of his uncle's in the Scottish Lowlands. After a series of mishaps, Edward eventually finds himself swept up into the Highlands where he becomes acquainted with the MacIvor clan chief, Fergus, and his beautiful sister, Flora. Edward is at first infatuated with the staunchly Jacobite Flora MacIvor, and, after meeting Charles Edward Stuart, is tempted to join the Jacobite cause. He eventually recognizes the error of his ways, however, when, as he sees and hears the English soldiers mounting their offensive at Prestonpans, he starts to identify the Highland troops as other: "It was at that instant, that, looking around him, he saw the wild dress and appearance of his Highland associates, heard their whispers in an uncouth and unknown language, looked upon his own dress, so unlike that which he had worn from his infancy, and wished to awake from what seemed at the moment a dream, strange, horrible, and unnatural."[206] At the conclusion of the novel, Edward ultimately realizes that his happiness lies in marrying Rose Bradwardine. In Scott's historical novel, Edward and Rose's union symbolizes a new future. Although the daughter of a Jacobite, Rose does not herself profess Jacobite principles; moreover, her father's Jacobite loyalty is represented as comic and antiquated rather than threatening. Those Jacobite figures who do constitute a political threat are eliminated from the novel: Fergus MacIvor is executed, and Flora moves to a convent in France. Edward's retrospective commentary on his adventures illustrates the stadial contours of the imaginative template that Scott proposes. Reflecting by the shores of Ullswater on his recent adventures, Edward identifies the Stuart cause with an exciting but unsustainable "romance" as he "felt himself entitled to say firmly, though perhaps with a sigh, that the romance of his life was ended, and that its real history had now commenced."[207] In *Waverley*, Scott demonstrates the appeal of the Jacobite cause and the power of Jacobite counter-memories, but ultimately identifies them with an earlier stage of society. Whereas Grant conceptualized a continuing important role for Highlanders in the present era, Scott's nostalgic perspective reshaped the Jacobite rising as part of Scotland's colorful history but a history that, like many other chapters, had to be concluded for the British nation to achieve modernity.

Despite's Scott's ideological promotion of progressive history and print culture, however, *Waverley* also suggests ways in which traces of the Jacobite past still linger, albeit in a changed form, in non-print media. Songs are particularly resonant in *Waverley*. Edward witnesses the impact of the song of the Scots Gaelic bard Mac-Murrough on the followers of Fergus MacIvor as well as experiencing its power himself in the translated version that Flora performs for him. The antic character David Gellatley, too, demonstrates the continuing importance of songs as he draws on a huge lyrical repertoire to communicate his oblique messages. Unlike Grant, however, who celebrated the importance of Highland oral culture and suggested the continuity of a Scottish Gaelic mediascape with different relative values, Scott presents Highland culture as more compromised and attenuated in *Waverley*. Flora herself indicates that the bardic song in its original form is "measured and monotonous"; her translation, however, which is crafted and performed to appeal to Edward's romantic expectations, creatively substitutes "a lofty and uncommon Highland air" for the original's "recitative."[208] David's songs are also broken pieces, intermingled with foreign songs as well. For Scott, modernity is both embodied in and achieved through a culture of print, represented by his narrator's references to the genre of the newspaper and his meta-narrative references to the construction of the novel itself.

---

[206] Scott, *Waverley*, p. 317. [207] Scott, *Waverley*, p. 385. [208] Scott, *Waverley*, p. 182.

As Rigney suggests, *Waverley* created a template for the historical novel form, "open[ing] up the past as an imaginative resource" and "inspiring a fashion for history as a key to collective identity that continues down to the present time."[209] Scott would go on to write variations on the historical novel template, including two more novels about the Jacobites, *Rob Roy* (1817) and *Redgauntlet* (1824). His popularization of Scottish history was made all the more effective because, as the works of the "Author of *Waverley*" became a literary phenomenon, the novels were remediated into other genres: from operatic performances to circus productions to illustrations.[210] Scott's work represents in itself a complex "knot of memory." Even as *Waverley* and the other Jacobite novels represent the lingering traces of Jacobite culture, their popularity contributed to a new fascination with the Highlands as Scott "invent[ed] the literary conditions for the next wave of Highland tourism," as Nigel Leask suggests.[211] Scott also encouraged the vogue for "Highlandism" by helping to orchestrate George IV's 1822 visit to Edinburgh, a pageant of tartan and performance of Highland culture which became known as "The King's Jaunt."[212]

Scott's success inspired other writers to turn to the Scottish past as "an imaginative resource." Christine Isobel Johnstone's *Clan-Albin: A National Tale* (1815) was published a year after *Waverley*, although, as Johnstone is quick to claim in her Advertisement, half of the novel actually appeared in print before Scott's novel. Where Scott narrativizes the memory of the Jacobites in an appealing way while suggesting their extinction, Johnstone takes up the troubling consequences of the 1745 rising, focusing on the current dispossession of the Highlanders in her tale of the "Lady" of Glen-albin and her clan. In the decade after *Waverley*, a number of other novels focused on the history of Scottish Jacobites were published.[213] David Carey's *Lochiel: or, The Field of Culloden* (1820), the anonymous *A Legend of Argyle: or, Tis a Hundred Years Since* (1821), and John Hervey Ashworth's *Hurstwood: A Tale of the Year 1715* (1823) share the political ideology of the Author of *Waverley*: "the assumption that Britain's post-Union, Hanoverian political settlement operated on enlightened principles of tolerance, freedom, and the benign rule of law."[214]

A very different perspective on the cultural memory of the Jacobites, and of cultural memory itself, however, is presented by James Hogg in his 1823 novel *The Three Perils of Woman*. In volume 3 of that work, Hogg relates the story of Sally Niven, a Lowlander whose husband, Alaster M'Kenzie, and former lover, Peter Gow, join the Jacobite cause. Hogg's description of the brutality of the government forces and the destruction of the landscape and its people echoes Smollett's *The*

---

209 Rigney, *Afterlives*, p. 4.   210 See Rigney, *Afterlives* and Buchanan, *Acts*.
211 Leask, *Stepping Westward*, p. 220.
212 See Coltman, *Art and Identity*; Duncan, *Scott's Shadow*; and Leask, *Stepping Westward*.
213 See Johnstone, *Clan-Albin*.   214 Mack, "Culloden," p. 99.

Tears of Scotland as Sally wanders by the battlefield at Culloden: "all was ruin and desolation. Hamlet, castle, and villa, had shared the same fate; all were lying in heaps of ashes, and not a soul to be seen save a few military, and stragglers of the lowest of adverse clans scraping up the poor wrecks of the spoil of an extirpated people."[215] Alaster and Peter are killed by Hanoverian soldiers, and Sally, who has witnessed their murders and has gone mad with grief, throws herself onto the corpse of her husband. Hogg interrupts the tragic and sentimental closure that such a narrative perspective might offer, however, as Sally is reanimated when an acquaintance, Davie Duff, who is working for the Duke of Cumberland, attempts to bury her and her husband. Sally revives, but then disappears. She is discovered nine months later singing in the snow and cradling an infant, but when help finally reaches her, both she and the child have perished. The cyclical format of Hogg's novel foregrounds the non-linear nature of memory while the narrator himself also comments self-consciously on the processes of cultural memory and forgetting: "There were many things happened to the valiant conquerors of the Highlands in 1746 that were fairly hushed up, there being none afterwards that dared to publish or avow them. But there is no reason why these should die. For my part, I like to rake them up whenever I can get a story that lies within twenty miles of them, and, for all my incidents, I appeal to the records of families, and the truth of history."[216] The narrator presents himself as a keeper of counter-memories, at the same time suggesting that "truth" lies not in official accounts, but in the domestic realm, in "records of families." Where Scott's *Waverley* ends with Edward Waverley nostalgically recalling his brief flirtation with the Jacobite cause as represented in the portrait of him in his tartan outfit together with Fergus MacIvor, Hogg, like Johnstone, focuses on the social and individual tragedies that followed the 1745 rising, noting, in conclusion, "Is there human sorrow on record like this that winded up the devastations of the Highlands?"[217]

The publication history of *The Three Perils of Woman* indicates the way in which the passing down of particular cultural memories requires not just initial storage through representation in print, but also continued circulation and access of the mediation. According to Douglas Mack, *The Three Perils of Woman* met with "shocked and hostile interest on its publication in 1823," but "after the 1820s it fell from sight for a century and a half" and was unavailable in print until 1995.[218] While not subject to the same erasure as Hogg's novel, *Clan-Albin* also fell by the wayside in the shadow of Scott, whose *Waverley* proved to be an enduring "object of recollection" in its own right, occluding or even displacing other cultural memories of the Jacobites.

---

215 Hogg, *Three Perils*, 3, p. 254.   216 Hogg, *Three Perils*, 3, p. 176.
217 Hogg, *Three Perils*, 3, p. 371.   218 Mack, "Culloden," p. 99.

3.7 Scottish Jacobite Songs and Relics

At the same time during which Scott's nostalgic representation of the Jacobites was undergoing an exponential growth in popularity, other re-activations of Jacobite memory were also circulating, particularly in the genre of song. William Donaldson credits the poet and songsmith Robert Burns with "single-handedly invent[ing] the Jacobite song as an independent type."[219] As indicated previously, songs were an important indicator of political affiliation in Jacobite circles during the earlier part of the eighteenth century. However, by adopting and adapting earlier lyrics or tunes, Burns, a Lowlander, did succeed in bringing Jacobitism into a shared Scottish national discourse. Burns's representation of Jacobitism is complex. In songs such as "It Was A' For Our Rightfu' King" and "O'er the Water to Charlie," for example, he celebrates the heroic exploits and the loyalty of the adherents of the Stuarts, affectively connecting contemporary audiences to their ideology.[220] But other songs, such as "Ye Jacobites by Name," are more ambiguous. Using the narrative voice of a Jacobite follower ostensibly lamenting his own and his cause's fate, Burns draws attention to the arbitrary relation between morality, law and political power ("What is Right and what is Wrang, by the law?") as well as to the nature of official cultural memory which is determined by the victors ("What makes heroic strife, fam'd afar?").[221] The song concludes on a double note, too, as the speaker's warning to "let your schemes alone" could be addressing either the Jacobite insurgents or the Hanoverian government "in the state" who won the victory and who are now scheming to claim the role of heroes. The reference to the "rising sun," a Jacobite image of restoration, is similarly at odds with the implication of the collapse of the Jacobite hopes. Despite, or perhaps because of such complex perspectives, Burns was keen to integrate his Jacobite songs, like his other lyric productions, into the canon of Scottish national song, including them in two important musical collections: James Johnson's *Scots Musical Museum* (1787–1803) and George Thomson's *A Select Collection of Scotish [sic] Melodies* (1793–1841). In the pages of these two collections, Burns provides a multifaceted Scottish identity, linking it to both Highland and Lowland cultural memories through his adoption of a range of voices.

Similarly important to establishing and promoting the genre of Jacobite songs as expressions of Scottish national identity is Carolina Oliphant, Lady Nairne. In Oliphant's case, sympathy for the Jacobite cause was more immediate as her parents had lost their estate and spent eighteen years in exile in France for their

---

[219] Donaldson, *Jacobite Songs*, p. 4.

[220] See "Songs Recorded to Complement *The Scots Musical Museum*," "Editing Robert Burns for the 21st Century," (University of Glasgow School for Critical Studies) for period recordings of Burns's songs.

[221] Kinsley, *Burns Poems and Songs*, p. 507.

role in the 1745 rising, returning in 1664, just two years before her birth (she was in fact named Carolina after the Stuart heir). Oliphant published all her work either anonymously or pseudonymously, contributing lyrics such as "The Auld House," "Wha'll Be King But Charlie?", "The Hundred Pipers" and "Will Ye No Come Back Again?" to Robert Purdie's *The Scotish [sic] Minstrel* (1821). It was not until after her death that her authorship of lyrics became known, as her work was published in *Lays from Strathearn* (1846). But Oliphant was not just a proponent of sentimental Jacobitism. As Juliet Shields points out, in her comic songs such as "Ye'll Mount, Gudeman" and "The Women have A' Gane Wud," Oliphant "uses dark humor to explore the range of women's experiences of the '45 and their investments in the Jacobite cause," providing a critical perspective both on politics and masculinity.[222] Both Burns's and Oliphant's Jacobite songs were further popularized in the expanding early nineteenth-century market for pianoforte music that focused on national traditions, and, as we will see, in the thriving chapbook marketplace, where their songs often appeared without attribution.[223]

Burns's and Oliphant's influence in reshaping Jacobite cultural memory into a more general Scottish national memory through song is clearly seen in the first published collection focusing specifically on Jacobite songs. James Hogg's *The Jacobite Relics* was commissioned in 1817 by the Highland Society of London with the help of George Thomson. Part one, published in 1819, contained "songs previous to the battle of Sheriffmuir," while the second, which appeared two years later, featured songs from the later historical period. Hogg also included Whig songs in the *Jacobite Relics*; however, as he himself asserted, they were not as appealing as the creative efforts of those supporting the Stuarts which "are the best that the country ever produced."[224] Hogg's poetic Dedication to "The Most Noble and Honorable President and Members of the Highland Society of London" praises "the sons of the men who ne'er flinched from their faith,/But stood for their sovereign to ruin and death." Like Campbell, Hogg focuses on the loyalty and bravery of the Jacobites who stood up for what they believed in, seeing them as individuals "Whom threat'ning ne'er daunted, nor power could dismay." In Hogg's representation, when the Jacobites finally "yielded, indignant, their necks to the blow,/Their homes to the flame, and their lands to the foe," the "wild strains" themselves flowed "to the rock and the wood," carrying the stories "Of the fall of the mighty, the Royal, and good."[225] Accordingly, the narrator presents himself as an intermediary, passing on the "Songs" as "memorials" that honor "the poets that sung, and the heroes that

---

[222] Shields, "Keeping It."   [223] See McAulay, *Our Ancient National Airs.*
[224] Hogg, *Jacobite Relics*, p. vii.   [225] Hogg, *Jacobite Relics*, p. v.

fell."[226] Although he represents his poetic avatar as a "Shepherd" who has a "Whiggish heart," Hogg also suggests that, through visiting the graves of the Jacobite heroes and wandering through the Highlands, that heart has become "knit to the Highlands" and "the cause they espoused to their cost." The poetic narrator also notes that he "grieved that the name of the STUART was lost!"[227]

Hogg's representation of the Jacobite songs, like Burns's, is ambiguous, however. On the one hand, he connects them with a hierarchical politics of nobility, lamenting the time "When kings were degraded, to ruffians a prey" and excoriating those who "turn up the snout of derision and scorn/At those who to honour or titles are born!"[228] On the other hand, he also associates the loss of the Stuart monarchy with the loss of a genuine nobleness of spirit. He notes "now there are myriads, the worst of the vile,/Whose highest ambition is bent to defame/All greatness and sovereignty, order and name!"[229] His animus is directed not against "beggars" per se, but against "beggarly power," and he ends his Dedication by "bequeath[ing]" his work to the current members of the Highland Society, whom he addresses as "Noble Highlanders," beseeching them to be as "loyal and gallant" as their "fathers."[230]

Hogg's presentation of the songs is similarly ambiguous. On the one hand, they are designated "relics" in the title, suggesting their interest as antiquarian objects, and Hogg loads them with copious notes including previous publication details as well as historical explanations of people and events of varying degrees of accuracy. On the other hand, he also suggests a recalibration that allows for a new kind of engagement with the material. *Jacobite Relics* provides music for most of the songs, encouraging consumers to sing the songs and, potentially, improvise their own accompaniment, as the music consists only of a melody line on a staff. He also ends his Introduction by requesting that his readers contribute to his future compilations, noting coyly that "A number of Charlie Stuart songs are still lacking, both Gaelic and English. May I hope that I shall have many others, both gentlemen and ladies, to add to my next list?"[231] Such an invitation to co-create the next installment of *Jacobite Relics* constitutes a collective act of remembrance in the present.

In the Introduction, Hogg voices his astonishment that the Jacobite songs haven't been collected previously. He suggests that the songs are useful for their official and unofficial capacity. They both provide a "rude epitome of the history of our country" during a period which formed a decisive chapter in the "establishment of the rights and liberties which we have since enjoyed"; and they also provide information about and for the families involved in the conflict, both

---

[226] Hogg, *Jacobite Relics*, p. v.   [227] Hogg, *Jacobite Relics*, p. vi.
[228] Hogg, *Jacobite Relics*, p. vi.   [229] Hogg, *Jacobite Relics*, p. vi.
[230] Hogg, *Jacobite Relics*, p. vi.   [231] Hogg, *Jacobite Relics*, p. xvi.

those who were "involved in ruin by the share they had in those commotions" and those who "rose on that ruin in consequence of the support they afforded to the side that prevailed."[232] Moreover, in Hogg's estimation, the songs symbolize resistance both in their content and their form. They represent a "rude energetic humour, that bids defiance to all opposition, in arms, sentiments, or rules of song-writing" and they are "the unmasked effusions of a bold and primitive race, who hated and despised the overturning innovations that prevailed in church and state."[233] As Murray Pittock points out, instead of representing a nostalgic view of the Jacobites of the past, Hogg's *Relics* "gave room to far too many aggressive and disturbing voices."[234]

The Jacobite Relics represented a deliberate desire on the part of the Highland Society to memorialize the past, to make the Jacobite cause into a *lieu de mémoire* in Pierre Nora's terms, but one which, like *Waverley*, would provide a sympathetic perspective on the Jacobites. In the enterprising, creative and canny hands of James Hogg, however, the project took on ambiguous overtones that in turn suggested that the Jacobite cause can only be understood in multiple, sometimes contradictory ways. Ultimately, Hogg upended the Highland Society of London's desire for a legitimate memorialization that, like Scott's *Waverley*, would establish a unified and progressive future for the British state while commemorating the valiant Jacobites of the past.

3.8 Irish Jacobite Songs

In the later eighteenth and early nineteenth centuries, examples of translations of Irish Gaelic Jacobite songs also began to be circulated by cultural brokers working between the traditions of Irish Gaelic and English literature. As we will see, these works demonstrate the many different political purposes to which Jacobite cultural memory was put. In her *Reliques of Irish Poetry* (1789), Charlotte Brooke, for example, included "Emon a Knock," or "Ned of the Hill" noting that the subject of the song, otherwise known as Edmond Ryan, "commanded a company of those unhappy free booters called Rapparees, who, after the defeat of the Boyne, were obliged to abandon their dwellings and possessions."[235] But Brooke omits any mention of the *aisling* aspect of "Emon a Knock," interpreting the song merely as a love story about Ned's "desertion" by his "mistress" and noting "I have not been able to discover the name of this fair inconstant."[236] While Brooke also included the original lyrics to the song in Irish Gaelic in her work, she downplays the connection of the material with political dissent.

---

[232] Hogg, *Jacobite Relics*, pp. vii–viii.   [233] Hogg, *Jacobite Relics*, p. viii.

[234] Pittock, *Poetry and Jacobite Politics*, p. 225.

[235] Brooke, *Reliques*, p. 205. For more on Brooke, see Davis, *Music*, ch. 3.

[236] Brooke, *Reliques*, p. 206.

In his *General Collection of the Ancient Irish Music* (1796), Edmund Bunting also included harp tunes associated with the Jacobite cause. Bunting had taken down these tunes during the 1792 Belfast Harp Festival from the playing of a handful of old harpists, several of whom, including one Dennis Hampson, had Jacobite affiliations. Two subsequent editions of Bunting's Irish music published under revised titles also featured Jacobite tunes from the Irish Gaelic tradition. *A General Collection of the Ancient Music of Ireland* (1809) acknowledges some Jacobite connections, as Bunting suggests, for example, that "Gye Fiane," or "The Wild Geese," was "sung as a farewell to the exiles after the capitulation of Limerick in 1691."[237] In *The Ancient Music of Ireland* (1840), however, Bunting's acknowledgment of the Jacobite origins of tunes such as "The Blackbird" and "Dear Black Cow" is limited to his inclusion of their original titles: "An Londubh" and "Druimin Dhubh" appear in the "Index to the Irish Names of the Airs."[238] Although Bunting, like Brooke, downplayed the political dissent of the songs, his collections of Irish music nevertheless stored the memory of the tunes, facilitating their transmission into the mainstream of traditional music.

The 1792 Belfast Harp Festival took place at the same time as another event in Belfast, the meeting of the Society of United Irishmen, an organization consisting of both Catholics and Protestants focused on promoting the democratic principles of the American and French Revolutions. In 1798, frustrated with the lack of political change in Ireland, members of the United Irishmen undertook their own rising against the British government. The Irish Rebellion, as it became officially known after its subsequent failure, was brutally suppressed. It also led to the complicated passing of the Acts of Union in the British and Irish parliaments in 1800, creating the United Kingdom of Great Britain and Ireland.[239]

Scholars have noted the overlap between Jacobite ideology as it was changing throughout the eighteenth century and ideas of political reform that were developing through organizations such as the United Irishmen who were sympathetic to the democratic revolutions in America and France. As Ó Buachalla observes, Jacobite poetry was originally "a conservative rhetoric imbued with the traditional values of aristocracy, hierarchy, hereditary right and social order"; at the same time, "it was also, potentially and eventually, a radical rhetoric in that it foretold, extolled and promoted the overthrow of the existing regime."[240] Both Jacobitism and the movement for democratic reform were based on challenging the political status quo. But, after the eruption of the Irish Rebellion in 1798, the rhetoric of democracy was more threatening to the British government than Jacobite politics. Ironically, in this climate, references

---

[237] For more on Bunting, see Davis, *Music*, ch. 4.

[238] Bunting, *Ancient Irish Music*, pp. ii–iii. For more on Bunting, see Davis, *Music*, ch. 4.

[239] See Jackson, *Two Unions*.   [240] Ó' Buachalla, "Irish Jacobite Poetry," p. 48.

to Jacobitism came to serve as a subversive code for democratic reform. In *Twelve Original Hibernian Songs* (1808), for example, Sidney Owenson signals a sympathy for reformist politics as she draws on several Jacobite tunes, providing new lyrics for them which revise the political message of Gaelic originals for the contemporary situation. In "Oh! farewell Dear Erin," which is set to the Jacobite tune "Drimenduath," Owensen draws on the association of Ireland with the female figure common in *aisling* poetry. The speaker of the song laments his state of exile, suggesting that he has been "forc'd from my love and my country," yet he notes that his "sad heart" is still held by "Eveline and Erin."[241] The subject of exile is here relevant both to the Jacobite followers of James Stuart who left their native land in 1691, as well as those who had left Ireland more recently after 1798 as a result of their efforts to secure political change in Ireland. The ambiguity inherent in Owenson's work also became a key feature of the *Irish Melodies* by Thomas Moore.[242] Like Owenson, Moore seeds his work with Jacobite influences, using Jacobite tunes for which he wrote new lyrics and employing the trope of the *aisling*.[243]

The use of Jacobite rhetoric to advocate for political reform in nineteenth-century Ireland is made explicit in James Hardiman's 1831 *Irish Minstrelsy; or, Bardic Remains of Ireland with English Poetical Translations*. In a section entitled "Jacobite Relics," Hardiman revises the association of the Irish with the Stuart cause, suggesting that Irish quickly realized the limitations of the Stuart monarchs. Although they continued to fight for James and his heirs, "it was more from a principle of allegiance, with, perhaps, a vain hope of regaining their freedom and confiscated estates, than from any particular attachment to him, or his ungrateful race."[244] Correspondingly, the Irish bards kept writing Jacobite verse because it was a vehicle that allowed them to pass on their sentiments "of political hope, enmity, revenge, or despair," giving them strength to imagine a way of throwing off their English oppressors. Hardiman suggests that Jacobite songs are now "remembered … more for the sake of the charming airs with which they are associated, than for any political sentiments which they may contain."[245] But he uses the discussion of Jacobite songs to convey a warning that, even though Ireland has been "rendered a paralyzed limb on the empire," it still possesses "sufficient nerve" by means of which, "in some frenzied or convulsive moment, it may inflict a sudden and deadly wound on the body which it ought to protect, support, and

---

[241] Owenson, *Twelve Original Hibernian Songs*, p. 13. For more on Owenson, see Davis, *Music*, ch. 5.

[242] For digital facsimiles of Moore's *Melodies*, see the Thomas Moore Project, Queen's University, Belfast.

[243] For more on Moore, see Davis, *Music*, ch. 6.   [244] Hardiman, *Irish Minstrelsy*, 2:7.

[245] Hardiman, *Irish Minstrelsy*, 2:8.

adorn."[246] Although Irish Jacobite songs may now be "harmless," Hardiman still uses their collection and curation to convey a powerful message regarding Irish disenfranchisement under English rule in 1831.

3.9 Performing Jacobitism in Nineteenth-Century Chapbooks

While literary works such as poetry, novels and song collections were important in recalibrating Jacobitism for the middling and upper ranks, chapbooks did the work of shaping Jacobitism for a growing working-class reading population in the nineteenth century.[247] This Element concludes therefore with a focus on chapbooks and cheap printed works, arguing that Jacobitism became an increasingly popular although entangled subject of cultural memory in the later eighteenth and early nineteenth centuries through becoming a staple of the chapbook and songster publications which functioned in a dynamic relation to more literary materials.

Anette Hagan observes that "nearly a century after the 1715 Rising, and perhaps six decades after the 1745, Jacobite content in chapbooks had become commonplace."[248] In fact, Jacobitism took on multiple identities in chapbook form as chapbooks condensed and combined material for the consumption of a newly expanding reading public, including a large working-class contingent. It is difficult to analyze chapbooks quantitatively because they were cheaply printed, and we can only draw on the material that remains in archives, but G. Ross Roy suggests as a "conservative estimate" that the sale of chapbooks from 1750 to 1850 amounted to "over 200,000 per year."[249] Hagan offers a sense of the chronological development of the political focus of chapbooks as she notes that the surviving chapbooks printed before 1770 were uniformly anti-Jacobite in tone, either because chapbook printers were wary of laws of sedition or because their readership, primarily from the Scottish Lowlands and England, supported the government side. After 1770, however, as she observes, the publication of pro-Jacobite items, particularly songs, increased. By the early nineteenth century, works from both political perspectives were circulating.

Hagan speculates that many of the pro-Jacobite songs that began to be printed in chapbooks after 1770 were transmitted through oral tradition before they came to be printed. In their original oral or manuscript contexts, such songs were affirmations of political affiliation. For the audiences who later consumed them in the eighteenth- and nineteenth-century chapbooks, however, the songs offered a connection to a general Scottish identity.[250] Jacobite songs by writers such as Burns, Oliphant and Hogg that had been written or adapted from earlier

---

[246] Hardiman, *Irish Minstrelsy*, 2:64   [247] See Cowan and Paterson, *Folk in Print*.
[248] Hagan, "Jacobite Chapbooks."   [249] Roy, "Some Notes," p. 50.
[250] See Kidd, "Rehabilitation."

songs were also popular items in later chapbooks, although they usually appear without acknowledgement of the author's name. Smollett's *The Tears of Scotland* also circulated anonymously in the nineteenth century in chapbook form in a publication titled *Three Excellent Songs* (see Figure 25), as did works like *The History of Prince Charles Edward Stuart Commonly Called The Pretender* (see Figure 26).

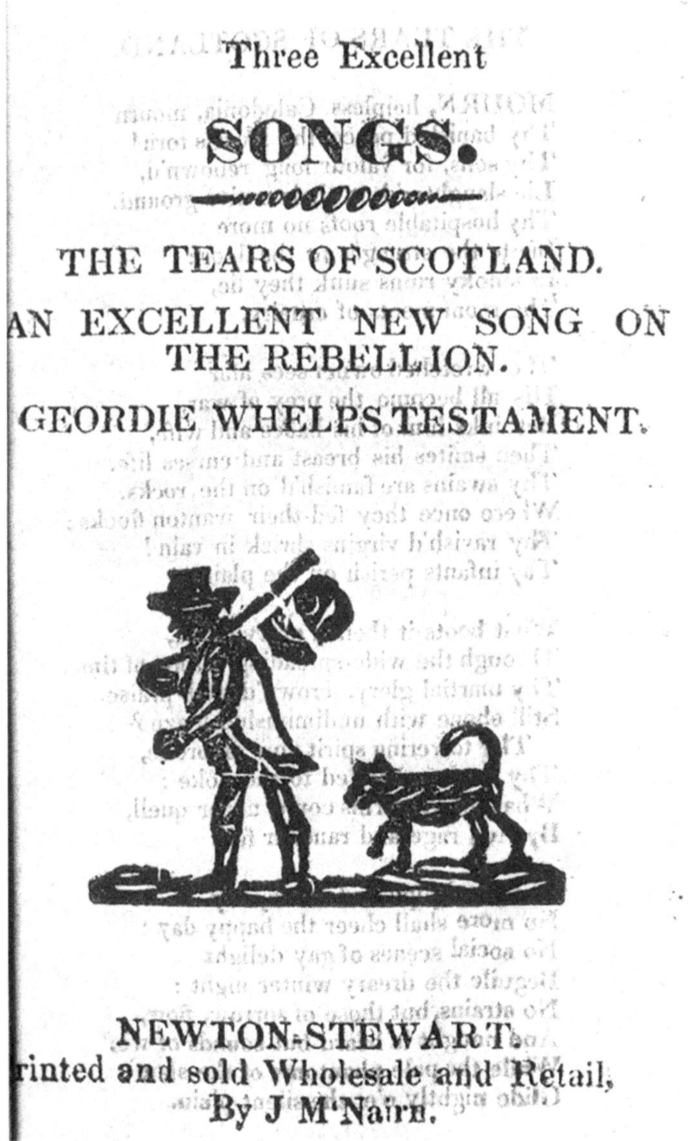

Figure 25 *Three Excellent Songs.* Scottish Chapbooks. Archival & Special Collections, University of Guelph. Public domain.

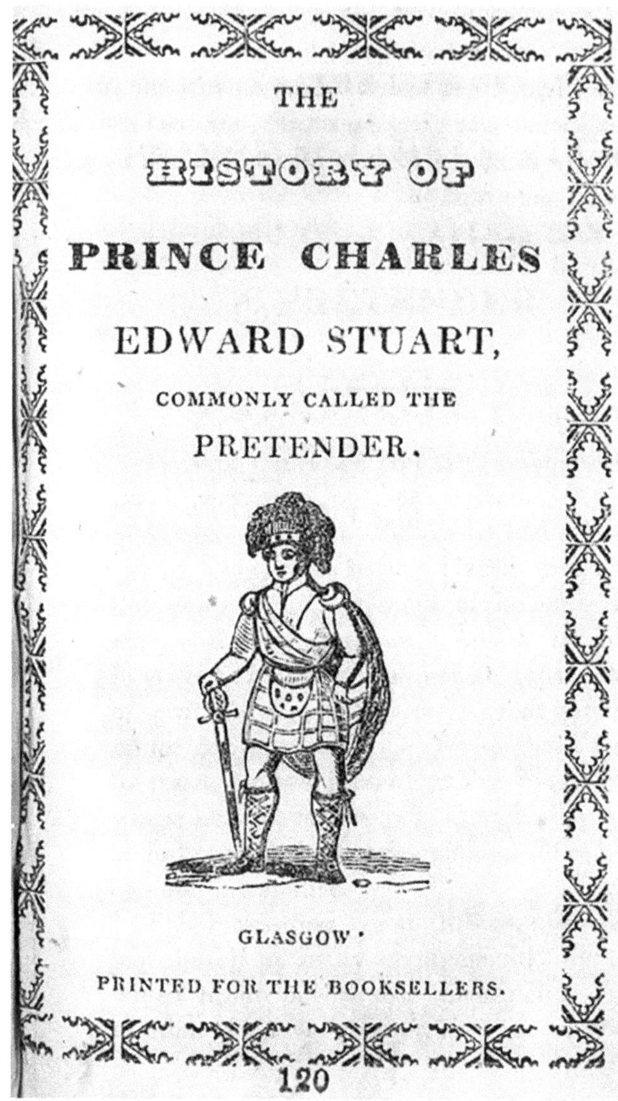

Figure 26 *The History of Prince Charles Edward Stuart Commonly Called The Pretender.* Scottish Chapbooks. Archival & Special Collections, University of Guelph. Public domain.

The latter work is generally positive about the Jacobites, relating in glowing terms the life of "this interesting young Prince" and even praising their decision to turn back at Derby as "one of the most surprising retreats, perhaps ever performed." The author further suggests that "They committed no outrage, and they were effectually restrained from the exercise of rapine."[251] The *History* follows the fortunes of

---

[251] *History of Prince Charles Edward Stuart*, pp. 3 and 10.

Charles Edward Stuart through the battle of Culloden and his escape, although it concludes with a negative perspective on his final years, noting that he "sunk into insignificance and oblivion."[252] On the pro-government side, Dougal Graham's *Account* went through two more editions during the author's lifetime (in 1752 and 1774) as well as six more posthumous editions by 1811, while the chapbook *Most Remarkable Passages in the Life of the Honorable Colonel James Gardiner* was also reprinted in several editions which still survive (see Figure 27; Gardiner was a government officer killed at Prestonpans). Chapbook readers were thus presented with diverse perspectives on the previous century's history.

A common feature of nineteenth-century chapbooks, however, is their lack of discrimination in terms of political affiliation. Like the earlier eighteenth-century popular works circulating after the 1745 rising, chapbooks were designed to sell copies, and printers therefore drew on a variety of materials. Because a number of chapbooks were composed of reproductions of a wide variety of materials within one volume, they frequently combine items expressing pro- and anti-Jacobite perspectives as well as general songs. The chapbook entitled *Five Popular Songs*, printed in Falkirk around 1825, for example, contains four pro-Jacobite songs and one general song (see Figure 28).

The pro-Jacobite "Culloden Day" is set just after the battle as the narrator addresses a "lady fair," directing her to "mourn the memory/Of all our Scottish fame" while he vows to protect her from exile or assault from Cumberland's troops.[253] "Hame, hame, hame!" is written from the perspective of a Jacobite exile who laments the death of "the great" and "the brave" who "attempted to save/The White Rose," while managing to remain hopeful about his own future and that of his nation as he observes that "the sun thro' the mist yearns to promise ta me,/I will shine on you yet in your ain contrie."[254] "Bonnie Charlie" and "Lewie Gordon," the two songs that conclude the chapbook, go back to the time before Culloden, as they express loyalty to Charles Edward Stuart and excitement about the prospect of being able to "welcome Bonnie Charlie" home. While these pro-Jacobite songs promote a hierarchy elevating the Stuart monarchy and their "great" followers, however, an earlier song, "Contented wi' Little," celebrates the happiness that comes with appreciating the simple pleasures in life. The speaker of this song suggests that contentment makes him independent from concerns about social rank: "my freedom's my lairdship nae monarch dare touch."[255] In this case, the chapbook fuses together different ideologies. Unlike the fusion that occurs in Scott's novels, however, this fusion does not include mapping political affiliation onto a progressive

---

[252] *History of Prince Charles Edward Stuart*, p. 25.   [253] *Five Popular Songs*, p. 2.
[254] *Five Popular Songs*, p. 5.   [255] *Five Popular Songs*, p. 5.

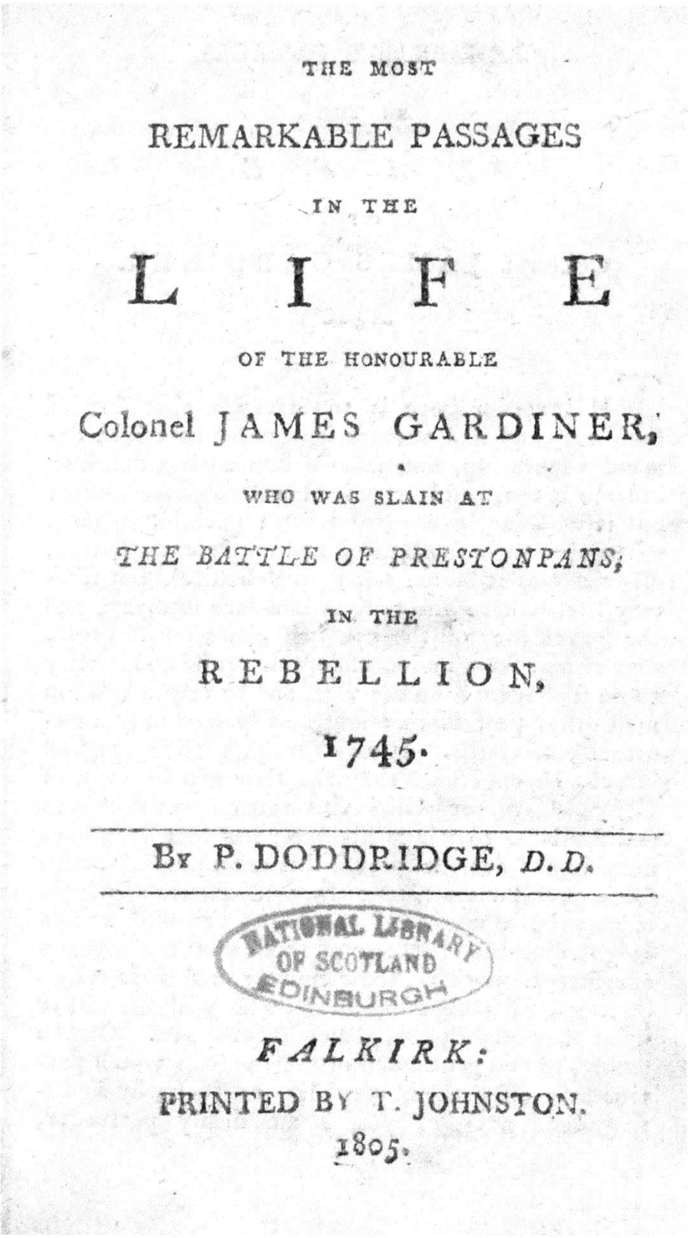

THE MOST

REMARKABLE PASSAGES

IN THE

L I F E

OF THE HONOURABLE

Colonel JAMES GARDINER,

WHO WAS SLAIN AT

THE BATTLE OF PRESTONPANS;

IN THE

R E B E L L I O N,

1745.

By P. DODDRIDGE, *D.D.*

FALKIRK:

PRINTED BY T. JOHNSTON.

1805.

Figure 27 *Most Remarkable Passages in the Life of the Honorable Colonel James Gardiner.* National Library of Scotland. Creative Commons 4.0.

history of the nation which nostalgizes the Jacobites. The chapbooks offer instead unresolved knots of memory that leave consumers to interpret and perform the past in the present in multiple ways.

Figure 28 *Five Popular Songs.* Scottish Chapbooks. Archival & Special Collections, University of Guelph. Public domain.

Much more research needs to be done on the social and literary contributions of chapbooks to Jacobite cultural memory. Like Scott's novels, the chapbooks and songsters were circulating at a crucial point in the history of the cultural memory of the Jacobites, as those individuals who had personal memories of the previous century's momentous events were passing or had already passed away. Robert

Chambers comments on the implications of this watershed moment for an understanding of Jacobitism in his *History of the Rebellion in Scotland, 1745, 1746* (1830), as he notes that, although the recollection of the 1745 rising "still excites so many feelings of a powerfully agitating nature in the bosoms of my countrymen," the "present generation" is now almost "entirely removed by distance of time from that of the ear and eye witnesses."[256] Indeed, whereas earlier figures such as Macpherson, Campbell, Grant, Burns, Oliphant, Scott and Hogg would all have had personally encountered individuals who had taken part in or who knew someone who had taken part in the last Jacobite rising, the generations following had no such direct access.[257] A closer exploration of chapbooks containing Jacobite material has the potential to further add to our understanding of the shaping of Jacobite cultural memory during this time of transition from what Assmann describes as "communicative" to "cultural memory.

4 Conclusion

In the 2021 issue of *Memory Studies,* editors Eneken Laanes and Hanna Meretoja suggest that "Dominant cultural memorial forms can be so self-evident that they are simply taken for granted, often only becoming visible when they are contested and brought to critical light by counter-memories."[258] This Element has examined the creation of anti-Jacobite memorial forms in the long eighteenth century as well as their re-activations and remediations in the late eighteenth and early nineteenth centuries in literary and popular printed genres. It has also focused on the continuing presence of counter-memories within those dominant narrative forms, despite attempts to eradicate them. It has argued that the shaping and re-shaping of Jacobitism within print culture and literary formations has occluded our understanding of the complexities of the history of the long eighteenth century. It is my hope that examining the complications of memory and forgetting to which the Jacobite cause has been subjected over this period might help us shed light on the ways in which other voices and perspectives have been and continue to be occluded by more dominant mediations of cultural memory.

---

[256] Chambers, *History,* p. vii.

[257] Assmann and Czaplicka, "Collective Memory," pp. 127–29).

[258] Laanes and Meretoja, "Editorial," p. 7.

Select Bibliography

A Diary of the Siege & Surrender of Lymerick: With the Articles at Large: Both Civil and Military. Dublin: Robert Thornton, 1692.

A Full Description of These Times, or the Prince of Orange's March from Exeter to London. London, 1689. English Broadside Ballad Archive. https://ebba.english.ucsb.edu/ballad/20870/album.

A Genuine Account of the Behaviour, Confession, and Dying Words, of Francis Townly [sic], (Nominal) Colonel of the Manchester Regiment, Thomas Deacon, James Dawson, John Barwick, George Fletcher and Andrew Blood. London, 1746. ECCO.

A Legend of Argyle: Or, Tis a Hundred Years Since. Vol. 1. London: G. & W. B. Whittaker, 1821.

A Narrative of the Whole Proceedings of Court at St. Margaret's Hill, Southwark. London, 1746.

ECCO. 2nd ed. https://archive.org/details/bim_eighteenth-century_an-authentick-narrative-_1746.

A New Touch of the Times, or, the Nations Consent for a Free Parliament. London, 1689. EBBA. https://ebba.english.ucsb.edu/ballad/22367/album.

A True Account of the Siege and Famous Defence Made at London-Derry. London, 1689.

Addison, Joseph. *The Free-Holder: Or, Political Essays*. London, 1716.

Alexis; or, the Young Adventurer: A Novel. London, 1746. https://archive.org/details/bim_eighteenth-century_alexis-or-the-young-ad_macdonald-alexander_1746.

An Account of the Proceedings and Transactions that Have Happened in the Kingdom of England, since the Arrival of the Dutch Fleet, and the Landing of the Prince of Orange's Army, &c.: As Also, the Progress the Prince Made; the Going Over to Him of the Mob. London, 1688.

An Authentick Narrative of the Whole Proceedings of Court at St. Margaret's Hill, Southwark. London, 1746.

Ascanius: Or, the Young Adventurer; a True History. London, 1746.

Asch, Ronald J. "The Hanoverian Monarchy and the Legacy of Late Stuart Kingship." In *The Hanoverian Succession: Dynastic Politics and Monarchical Culture*, edited by Andreas Gestrich and Michael Schaich, 25–41, German Historical Institute. London: Ashgate, 2015.

Assmann, Aleida. *Cultural Memory and Western Civilization: Functions, Media, Archives*. Cambridge: Cambridge University Press, 2011.

Assmann, Jan. *Cultural Memory and Early Civilization Writing, Remembrance, and Political Imagination*. Cambridge: Cambridge University Press, 2011.

Assmann, Jan, and John Czaplicka. "Collective Memory and Cultural Identity." *New German Critique*, no. 65 (1995): 125–33.

Aston, Nigel, and Benjamin Bankhurst, eds. *Negotiating Toleration: Dissent and the Hanoverian Succession, 1714–1760*. Oxford: Oxford University Press, 2019.

Bal, Mieke. *Travelling Concepts in the Humanities: A Rough Guide*. Toronto: University of Toronto Press, 2002.

Barker, Jane. "A Collection of Poems Referring to the Times since the King's Accession to the Crown, Occasionally writ According to the Circumstance of Time and Place." *Defining Gender 1450–1910: Five Centuries of Advice Literature Online*. Adam Matthew Online, 2005.

Beattie, William. *The Life and Letters of Thomas Campbell*, 3 vols. London: Edward Moxon, 1849.

Beek, J. *The Triumphs of William III: King of England, Scotland, France and Ireland*. London, 1702.

Black, Ronnie. "Alasdair mac Mhaighstir Alasdair and the New Gaelic Poetry." In *The Edinburgh History of Scottish Literature Volume Two: Enlightenment, Britain and Empire (1707–1918)*, edited by Susan Manning, 110–124. Edinburgh: Edinburgh University Press, 2007.

Black, Ronnie, ed. *An Lasair: An Anthology of 18th Century Scottish Gaelic Verse*. Edinburgh: Birlinn, 2001.

Black, Ronnie. *The Campbells of the Ark: Men of Argyll in 1745*. 2 vols. Edinburgh: Birlinn, 2016.

Bohun, Edward. The History of the Desertion. London, 1689.

Boswell, James. *The Journal of a Tour of the Hebrides*. London, 1785.

Bowie, Karen. *Public Opinion in Early Modern Scotland, c. 1560–1707*. Cambridge: Cambridge University Press, 2020.

Boyer, Abel. *The History of King William the Third: In III Parts*. London, 1702–03.

Briggs, Asa, and Peter Burke. *A Social History of Media: From Gutenberg to the Internet*. Malden: Blackwell, 2001.

Brooke, Charlotte. *Reliques of Irish Poetry*. Dublin: George Bonham, 1789.

Brown, Michael. "Jacobite Baroque and the Conspiratorial Mind." In *Shaping Jacobitism: 1688 to the Present: Memory, Culture, Networks*, edited by Leith Davis, and Kevin James. Edinburgh: Edinburgh University Press, in press.

Brownlees, Nicholas, ed. *The Edinburgh History of the British and Irish Press: Volume 1, Beginnings and Consolidation 1640–1800*. Edinburgh: Edinburgh University Press, 2023.

Buchanan, David. *Acts of Modernity: The Historical Novel and Effective Communication, 1814–1901*. London: Routledge, 2017.

Bunting, Edmund. *A General Collection of the Ancient Irish Music*. London, 1796.

Burnet, Gilbert. *A Compleat History of the Glorious Life and Reign of the Most Renowned Monarch, William the Third*. London, 1702. ECCO.

Calder, George. *The Gaelic Songs of Duncan MacIntyre/Orain Ghaidhealach le Donnchadh Macantsaoir*. Edinburgh: John Grant, 1912.

Campbell, John Lorne. *Highland Songs of the Forty-Five*. Edinburgh: John Grant, 1933; reprinted Edinburgh: Scottish Academic Press, 1984.

Campbell, Thomas. *The Pleasures of Hope, with Other Poems*. London: T. Bensley, 1803.

Carey, David. *Lochiel: Or, the Field of Culloden*. Vol. 1, London: George and William Budd Whittaker, 1820.

Chambers, Robert. *The History of the Rebellion in Scotland in 1745, 1746*. Edinburgh: Constable, 1830.

Chambers, Robert. *Jacobite Memoirs of the Rebellion of 1745*. Edinburgh: William and Robert Chambers, 1834.

Chambers, Robert. *Select Writings of Robert Chambers: History of the Rebellion of 1745–46*. Edinburgh: William and Robert Chambers, 1840.

Charles, P. R. *Jacobite Relics*. MS. 2960. f. 97 r. Edinburgh: National Library of Scotland, 2.

Clancy, Thomas. "Gaelic Literature and Scottish Romanticism." In *The Edinburgh Companion to Scottish Romanticism*, edited by Murray Pittock, 49–60. Edinburgh: Edinburgh University Press, 2011.

Clark, Jonathan Charles Douglas. *English Society 1688–1832: Ideology, Social Structure and Political Practice during the Ancien Regime*. Cambridge: Cambridge University Press, 2000.

Clyde, Robert. *From Rebel to Hero: The Image of the Highlander, 1745–1830*. East Linton: Tuckwell, 1995.

Coltman, Viccy. *Art and Identity in Scotland: A Cultural History from the Jacobite Rising of 1745 to Walter Scott*. Cambridge: Cambridge University Press, 2019.

A Compleat and Authentick History of the Rise, Progress and Extinction of the Late Rebellion. London, 1747.

Constantine, Mary-Ann, and Nigel Leask. "Introduction: Romanticism, Travel, and the Celtic Languages." *Studies in Romanticism*, vol. 63, no. 2 (2024): 97–115.

Corp, Edward T. *A Court in Exile: The Stuarts in France, 1689–1718*. Cambridge: Cambridge University Press, 2004.

Cowan, Edward, and Michael Paterson, eds. *Folk in Print: Scotland's Chapbook Heritage, 1750–1850*. Edinburgh: John Donald, 2007.

Cranfield, Geoffrey. *The Development of the Provincial Newspaper, 1700–1760*. Oxford: Clarendon Press, 1962.

Davis, Leith. *Acts of Union: Scotland and the Literary Negotiation of the British Nation, 1707–1830*. Stanford: Stanford University Press, 1998.

Davis, Leith. *Mediating Cultural Memory in Britain and Ireland*. Cambridge: Cambridge University Press, 2022.

Davis, Leith. "Memory Studies and the Eighteenth Century." *Literature Compass*, vol. 16, no. 2 (2019): 1–13. https://doi.org/10.1111/lic3.12504.

Davis, Leith. *Music, Postcolonialism, and Gender: The Construction of Irish National Identity, 1724–1874*. Notre Dame: University of Notre Dame Press, 2006.

Davis, Leith. "Rehabilitating Jacobites in Romantic-Era Britain: The Cultural Memory of the 1745 Rising in Thomas Campbell's 'Lochiel's Warning' and Anne Grant's 'The Highlanders'." In *Seeking Justice: Literature, Law and Equity during the Age of Revolutions*, edited by Regina Hewitt, and Michael Demson, 113–132. Edinburgh: Edinburgh University Press.

Davis, Leith, and Kevin James. *Shaping Jacobitism, 1688 to the Present: Memory, Culture, Networks*. Edinburgh: Edinburgh University Press, in press.

Davis, Leith and Laura Mottiez. "'Restory-ing" the Rightful King? Recycling and Revising Eighteenth-Century Cultural Memories of the Jacobites in Outlander' in *Shaping Jacobitism, 1688 to the Present: Memory, Culture, Networks*, edited by Leith Davis and Kevin James. Edinburgh: Edinburgh University Press, in press.

Defoe, Daniel. *The History of the Union of Great Britain*. Edinburgh, 1709.

Defoe, Daniel. *The Union-Proverb*. London, 1708.

Devine, Thomas. *Clanship to Crofters' War: The Social Transformation of the Scottish Highlands*. Manchester: Manchester University Press, 1994.

Donaldson, William. *Jacobite Song: Political Myth and National Identity*. Aberdeen: Aberdeen University Press, 1988.

Dryden, John. *The Works of Virgil Containing His Pastorals, Georgics and Aeneis: Adorn'd with a Hundred Sculptures Translated into English Verse by Mr. Dryden*. London, 1697.

Duncan, Ian. *Scott's Shadow: The Novel in Romantic Edinburgh*. Princeton, NJ: Princeton University Press, 2007.

Eicke, Leigh A. "Jane Barker's Jacobite Writings." In *Women's Writing and the Circulation of Ideas: Manuscript Publication in England, 1550–1800*, edited by Nathan Tinker, 137–157. Cambridge: Cambridge University Press, 2002.

Erll, Astrid. *Memory in Culture*. Translated by Sara B. Young. London: Palgrave Macmillan, 2011.

Erll, Astrid, and Ann Rigney. *Mediation, Remediation, and the Dynamics of Cultural Memory*. Berlin: de Gruyter, 2009.

Evans, Geraint, and Helen Fulton. "Introduction." In *The Cambridge History of Welsh Literature*, edited by Geraint Evans, and Helen Fulton, 1–10. Cambridge: Cambridge University Press, 2019.

Five Popular Songs:Culloden Day. Hame, hame, hame. Bonnie Charlie. Contented wi' little. Lewie Gordon. Scottish Chapbooks. https://scottishchap books.lib.uoguelph.ca/items/show/764.

A Full Collection of All the Proclamations and Orders, Published by the Authority of Charles, Prince of Wales, n.p., Glasgow, 1745. ECCO.

Forbes, Robert. "The Lyon in Mourning." Manuscript Digital Project, https:// lim.dhil.lib.sfu.ca.

Fox, Adam. *The Press and the People: Cheap Print and Society in Scotland, 1500–1785*. Oxford: Oxford University Press, 2020.

Grant, Anne. *Poems on Various Subjects*. J. Moir: Edinburgh, 1803.

Greenblatt, Stephen, James Noggle, Courtney Weiss Smith. *Norton Anthology of English Literature*. Volume C: Restoration and Eighteenth Century. 11th ed. New York: Norton, 2024.

Greenblatt, Stephen, Julie Orlemanski, Courtney Weiss Smith, et al. *Norton Anthology of English Literature*. Vol. 1. https://wwnorton.com/books/ 9781324062929.

Guthrie, Neil. *The Material Culture of the Jacobites*. Cambridge: Cambridge University Press, 2013.

Hagan, Anette. "Jacobite Chapbooks." In *Shaping Jacobitism: 1688 to the Present: Memory, Culture, Networks*, edited by Leith Davis, and Kevin James. Edinburgh: Edinburgh University Press, in press.

Hagan, Anette. "Reading the News in Scotland: The Jacobite Rising of 1715." In *The Edinburgh History of the British and Irish Press, Vol. I, 1640–1800*, edited by Nicholas Brownlee, 280–84. Edinburgh: Edinburgh University Press, 2023.

Hardiman, James. *Irish Minstrelsy; or, Bardic Remains of Ireland with English Poetical Translations*. 2 Volumes. London: Joseph Robbins, 1831.

Harris, Bob. "'A Great Palladium of Our Liberties': The British Press and the 'Forty-Five'." *Historical Research*, vol. 68, no. 165 (1995): 67–87.

Harris, Tim. *Revolution: The Great Crisis of the British Monarchy, 1685–1720*. London: Penguin, 2006.

Haywood, Eliza Fowler. *The Parrot: With a Compendium of the Times*. London, 1746. ECCO.

Henderson, Andrew. *The Edinburgh History of the Late Rebellion, MDCCXLV and MDCCXLVI*. London, 1752.

Henderson, Andrew. *A History of the Rebellion, 1745 and 1746: Containing a full Account of Its Rise, Progress and Extinction*. London, 1748.

The History of the Rebellion Raised against His Majesty King George II from Its Rise in August 1745, to Its Happy Extinction. Dublin, 1746.

The History of Prince Charles Edward Stuart, Commonly Called the Pretender. Scottish Chapbooks, https://scottishchapbooks.lib.uoguelph.ca/items/show/585.

Hogg, James. *The Jacobite Relics: Vol. 1*. Edited by Murray G. H. Pittock. Edinburgh: Edinburgh University Press, 2016. Oxford Scholarly Editions. Romantics Poetry Online. 10.1093/actrade/9780748615926.book.1.

Hogg, James. *The Three Perils of Woman*. Edinburgh: James Ballantyne, 1823.

Hone, Joseph. *Alexander Pope in the Making*. Oxford: Oxford University Press, 2021.

Hopkins, Paul. *Glencoe and the End of the Highland War*. Edinburgh: John Donald, 1986.

Horejsi, Nicole. *Novel Cleopatras: Romance Historiography and the Dido Tradition in English Fiction, 1688–1785*. Toronto: University of Toronto Press, 2019.

J.A. *Princely Excellency: Or, Regal Glory. Being an Exact Account of the Most Glorious Heroick, and Matchless Actions, of That Most Serene and Potent Prince, William the Third*. London, 1702. ECCO.

Jackson, Alvin. *The Two Unions: Ireland, Scotland, and the Survival of the United Kingdom, 1707–2007*. Oxford: Oxford University Press, 2012.

James II. *By the King, a Proclamation*. London, 1688.

Jenkins, Henry, Sam Ford, and Joshua Green. *Spreadable Media Creating Value and Meaning in a Networked Culture*. New York: New York University Press, 2013.

Johnstone, Christine Isobel. *Clan-Albin: A National Tale*. 3 vols. London: Longman, Hurst, Rees, Orme & Brown, 1815.

A Journey through Part of England and Scotland: Along with the Army under the Command of His Royal Highness the Duke of Cumberland. London, 1746.

Keegan, Bridget, and Libby Hallgren Hoxmeier. "Jane Barker's Catholic Poems: An Edition of 'Poems Refering to the Times' from the Magdalen Manuscript, Part One." *Tulsa Studies in Women's Literature*, vol. 31, no. 1 (2012): 181–228.

Kerrigan, John. *Archipelagic English: Literature, History, Politics, 1603–1707*. Oxford: Oxford University Press, 2008.

Kidd, Colin. "The Rehabilitation of Scottish Jacobitism," *Scottish Historical Review*, vol. 77 (1998): 58–76.

King, Rachael Scarborough, ed. *After Print: Eighteenth-Century Manuscript Cultures*. Charlottesville, VA: University of Virginia Press, 2020.

King, Rachael Scarborough. *Writing to the World: Letters and the Origins of Modern Print Genres*. Baltimore: Johns Hopkins University Press, 2018.

Kinsley, James. *Burns Poems and Songs*. Oxford: Oxford University Press, 1986.

Laanes, Eneken, and Hanna Meretoja. "Editorial: Cultural Memorial Forms." *Memory Studies* vol. 14, no. 1 (2021): 3–9.

Leask, Nigel. *Stepping Westward: Writing the Highland Tour, 1720–1830*. Oxford: Oxford University Press, 2020.

Lenihan, Pádraig, and Keith Sidwell. *Poema de Hibernia: A Jacobite Latin Epic on the Williamite Wars*. Dublin: Irish Manuscripts Commission, 2018.

Lenman, Bruce. *The Jacobite Risings in Britain, 1689–1746*. London: Eyre Methuen, 1980.

Levy, Michelle, and Betty A. Schellenberg. *How and Why to Do Things with Eighteenth-Century Manuscripts*. Cambridge: Cambridge University Press, 2021.

The Life, Adventures, and Many and Great Vicissitudes of Fortune of Simon, Lord Lovat. London, 1746.

MacCoinnich, Aonghas. "Clanship, Faith and Jacobitism: A Scottish Gaelic Poetry Collection, 1688–93." In *Shaping Jacobitism: 1688 to the Present: Memory, Culture, Networks*, edited by Leith Davis, and Kevin James. Edinburgh: Edinburgh University Press, in press.

Mac Mhaighstir Alasdair, Alasdair. *Ais-eiridh na Sean Chánoin Albannaich*. Duneidiunn/Edinburgh, 1751. https://digital.nls.uk/rare-items-in-gaelic/arch ive/114544436#?c=0&m=0&s=0&cv=4&xywh=-879%2C-110%2C2958% 2C2193.

Macinnes, Allan L. *Clanship, Commerce, and the House of Stuart, 1603–1788*. East Linton: Tuckwell, 1996.

Mack, Douglas S. "Culloden and After: Scottish Jacobite Novels." *Eighteenth-Century Life*, vol. 20, no. 3 (1996): 92–106.

Mackillop, Andrew. *More Fruitful than the Soil: Army, Empire and the Scottish Highlands 1715–1815*. East Linton: Tuckwell Press, 2000.

Macpherson, James. *Fingal, an Ancient Epic Poem*. London: T. Becket and P. A. De Hondt, 1762.

MacQueen, Jack. "From Rome to Ruddiman: The Scoto-Latin Tradition." In *The Edinburgh History of Scottish Literature I: From Columba to the Union (until 1707)*, edited by Thomas Owen Clancy and Murray Pittock, 184–208. Edinburgh: Edinburgh University Press, 2006.

Marchant, John. *The History of the Present Rebellion*. London, 1746.

McAulay, Karen. *Our Ancient National Airs: Scottish Song Collecting from the Enlightenment to the Romantic Era*. London: Routledge, 2013.

McDowell, Paula. "Media and Mediation in the Eighteenth Century." In *Oxford Handbook Topics in Literature*. Online ed., Oxford Academic. https://doi .org/10.1093/oxfordhb/9780199935338.013.46.

McGuirk, Carol. "Jacobite History to National Song: Robert Burns and Carolina Oliphant (Baroness Nairne)." *The Eighteenth Century*, vol. 47, no. 2/3 (2006): 253–87.

McLynn, Frank. *The Jacobites*. London: Routledge & Kegan Paul, 1985.

McNeil, Kenneth. *Scotland, Britain, Empire: Writing the Highlands, 1760–1860*. Columbus: Ohio State University Press, 2007.

Memoirs of the Life of Lord Lovat. London, 1746.

Millen, Graeme Stephen. *The Scots-Dutch Brigade and the Highland War, 1689–1691*. Doctor of Philosophy (PhD) thesis, University of Kent. 2022.

Monod, Paul Kléber. *Jacobitism and the English People, 1688-1788*. Cambridge: Cambridge University Press, 1993.

Morley, Vincent. "Irish Jacobitism, 1691–1790." *The Cambridge History of Ireland*. Vol. 3, edited by James Kelly, 23–47. Cambridge: Cambridge University Press, 2018.

Multigraph Collective. *Interacting with Print: Elements of Reading in the Era of Print Saturation*. Chicago: University of Chicago Press, 2018.

Nora, Pierre, and Lawrence D. Kritzman. *Realms of Memory: Rethinking the French Past*. New York: Columbia University Press, 1996.

Ó Buachalla, Breandán. "Irish Jacobite Poetry." *The Irish Review*, no. 12 (1992): 40–49. https://doi.org/10.2307/29735642.

Ó Ciardha, Éamonn. *Ireland and the Jacobite Cause, 1685–1766: A Fatal Attachment*. Dublin: Four Courts Press, 2001.

Ó Ciosáin, Niall. "The Language of the Printing-House: Why so Many Books in Welsh and Scottish Gaelic Were Printed in 18th-Century Ireland, and so Few in Irish." *Folk Life*, vol. 59, no. 1 (2021): 36–51.

Ó Ciosáin, Niall. *Print and the Celtic Languages: Publishing and Reading in Irish, Welsh, Gaelic and Breton, 1700–1900*. London: Routledge, 2024.

Ó Rathaille , Aodhagán. *"Gile na Gile"/"Brightness of Brightness."* Translated Brian O'Connor. *Irish Literary Society*. https://irishlitsoc.org/gile-na-gile/.

Ó Tuama, Seán. *Reposessions: Selected Essays on the Irish Literary Heritage*. Cork: Cork University Press, 1995.

Owenson, Sidney. *Twelve Original Hibernian Songs*. London: Preston, 1808.

Perkins, Pam. "The 'Candour, which Can Feel for a Foe': Romanticizing the Jacobites in the Mid-Eighteenth Century." *Lumen* vol. 31 (2012): 131–43.

Perkins, Pam. "Anne Grant and the Social Networks of Jacobitism" in *Shaping Jacobitism: 1688 to the Present: Memory, Culture, Networks*, edited by Leith Davis, and Kevin James. Edinburgh: Edinburgh University Press, in press.

Philp, James. "Panurgi Philocaballi Scoti Grameidos." MS. 100. Edinburgh: National Library of Scotland, 1691.

Philp, James. "Panurgi Philo-Cabelli-Scoti Grameidos." MS. 318. Edinburgh: National Library of Scotland, 1730.

Pittock, Murray. *Culloden: (Cuil Lodair)*. Oxford: Oxford University Press, 2016.

Pittock, Murray. *Material Culture and Sedition, 1688–1760: Treacherous Objects, Secret Places*. Houndmills: Palgrave Macmillan, 2013.

Pittock, Murray. *Poetry and Jacobite Politics in Eighteenth-Century Britain and Ireland*. Cambridge: Cambridge University Press, 1994.

Pittock, Murray. "New Jacobite Songs of the Forty-five." *Studies in Voltaire and the Eighteenth Century*, vol. 267 (1989): 1–75.

Pittock, Murray. *The Myth of the Jacobite Clans: The Jacobite Army in 1745*. Edinburgh: Edinburgh University Press, 2009. 2nd edition.

Pittock, Murray. "Scottish Song and the Jacobite Cause." In *The Edinburgh History of Scottish Literature*, edited by Ian Brown, Thomas Clancy, Susan Manning, and Murray Pittock, 105–9. Edinburgh: Edinburgh University Press, 2022.

Plank, Geoffrey. *Rebellion and Savagery: The Jacobite Rising of 1745 and the British Empire*. Philadelphia: University of Pennsylvania Press, 2006.

Pope, Alexander. *Windsor-Forest: To the Right Honourable George Lord Landsdown*. London, 1713.

Raffe, Alasdair. *Scotland in Revolution, 1685–1690*. Edinburgh: Edinburgh University Press, 2018.

Raven, James. "Non-metropolitan Printing and Business in Britain and Ireland between the Sixteenth and Eighteenth Centuries." In *Print Culture Histories beyond the Metropolis*, edited by James J. Connolly, Patrick Collier, Frank Felsenstein, Kenneth R. Hall and Robert Hall, 19–53. Toronto: University of Toronto Press, 2016.

Rigney, Ann. *The Afterlives of Walter Scott: Memory on the Move*. Oxford: Oxford University Press, 2012.

Rigney, Ann. "The Dynamics of Remembrance: Texts between Monumentality and Morphing." In *Cultural Memory Studies: An International and Interdisciplinary Handbook*, edited by Astrid Erll and Ansgar Nünning, 345–53. Berlin: De Gruyter, 2008.

Rogers, Pat. *Johnson and Boswell: The Transit of Caledonia*. Oxford: Clarendon Press, 1995.

Rorke, Mary Gordon. *A Full, Particular and True Account of the Rebellion in the Years 1745–6 by Dougal Graham*. MLitt(R) thesis, University of Glasgow, 2017.

Rothberg, Michael. "Introduction: Between Memory and Memory: From Lieux de Mémoire to Noeuds de Mémoire." *Yale French Studies*, no. 118/119 (2010): 3–12.

Roy, G. Ross. "Some Notes on Scottish Chapbooks." *Scottish Literary Journal*, vol. 1 (1974): 50–60.

Russell, Gillian. *The Ephemeral Eighteenth Century*. Cambridge: Cambridge University Press, 2020.

Sankey, Margaret. *Jacobite Prisoners of the 1715: Preventing and Punishing Insurrection in Early Hanoverian Britain*. Burlington, VT: Ashgate, 2005. p. xiii.

Schellenberg, Betty. *Literary Coteries and the Making of Modern Print Culture, 1740–1790*. Cambridge: Cambridge University Press, 2016.

Schwoerer, Lois. *The Declaration of Rights, 1689*. Baltimore: Johns Hopkins University Press, 1981.

Schwoerer, Lois. "Liberty of the Press and Public Opinion, 1660–1695." In *Liberty Secured?: Britain Before and After 1688*, edited by J. R. Jones, 199–230. Stanford: Stanford University Press, 1992.

Scott, Walter. *Waverley*. Edited by Susan Kubica Howard. Calgary: Broadview, 2010.

Seasonable Considerations on the Present War in Scotland. London, 1746.

Seton, Bruce Gordon, and Jean Gordon Arnot. *Prisoners of the '45*. Edinburgh: Edinburgh University Press by T. and A. Constable for the Scottish History Society, 1928.

Shields, Juliet. *Sentimental Literature and Anglo-Scottish Identity, 1745–1820*. Cambridge: Cambridge University Press, 2010.

Shields, Juliet. "Keeping It in the Family: Women's Perspectives on the '45." *Shaping Jacobitism, 1688 to the Present: Memory, Culture, Networks*. Edinburgh: Edinburgh University Press, in press.

Sirota, Brent S., and Allan I. Macinnes, eds. *The Hanoverian Succession in Great Britain and Its Empire*. Martlesham: The Boydell Press, 2019.

Siskin, Clifford, and William Warner. "This is Enlightenment: An Invitation in the Form of an Argument." In *This Is Enlightenment*, edited by Clifford Siskin and William Warner. Chicago: University of Chicago Press, 2010.

Smollett, Tobias. *The Tears of Scotland*. London? 1746? https://archive.org/details/bim_eighteenth-century_the-tears-of-scotland_smollett-tobias-george_1746/page/n3/mode/2up.

Steele, Richard. *The Town Talk, the Fish Pool, the Plebian, the Old Whig, the Spinster, &c.* London: Printed by John Nichols, 1790.

Stiùbhart, Domhnall Uilleam. "Adaptation, Integration, and Renewal: Scottish Gaelic Literature, 1650–1750." In *The International Companion to Scottish Literature of the Long Eighteenth Century*, edited by Leith Davis and Janet Sorensen, 24–40. Glasgow: Association for Scottish Literary Studies, 2021.

Stiùbhart, Domhnall Uilleam. "Gaelic Enlightenment to Global Gaelosphere: Gaelic Literature, 1750–1800." In *The International Companion to Scottish Literature of the Long Eighteenth Century*, edited by Leith Davis and Janet Sorensen, 149–169. Glasgow: Association for Scottish Literary Studies, 2021.

Szechi, Daniel. *1715: The Great Jacobite Rebellion*. New Haven: Yale University Press, 2006.

Szechi, Daniel. "The Jacobite Movement." In *A Companion to Eighteenth-Century Britain*, edited by Harry Thomas Dickinson, 81–96. Oxford: Blackwell, 2002. https://doi.org/10.1002/9780470998885.ch7.

Taylor, Edward. "Jacobites and Latin Verse, 1688–1702." *Journal for Eighteenth-Century Studies*, vol. 45, no. 4 (2022): 407–26.

Thomson, Derick. *An Introduction to Gaelic Poetry*. Edinburgh: Edinburgh University Press, 1990.

Thomson, Derick S. "Gaelic Poetry in the Eighteenth Century: The Breaking of the Mould." In *A History of Scottish Literature vol. 2 1660–1800*, edited by Andrew Hook, 175–90. Aberdeen: Aberdeen University Press, 1987.

Three Excellent Songs. The Tears of Scotland. An Excellent New Song on the Rebellion. Geordie Whelps Testament." *Scottish Chapbooks*, https://scottishchapbooks.lib.uoguelph.ca/items/show/809.

Trumpener, Katie. *Bardic Nationalism: The Romantic Novel and the British Empire*. Princeton, NJ: Princeton University Press, 1997.

The Tryals of William, Earl of Kilmarnock, George, Earl of Cromertie [sic], and Arthur Lord Balmerino, for High Treason. London, 1746.

The Wanderer, or Surprizing Escape. London, 1747.

Whatley, Christopher. *The Scots and the Union: Then and Now*. Edinburgh: Edinburgh University Press, 2014.

Wilkinson, W. *Trials of the Rebel Lords: A Compleat History of the Trials of the Rebel Lords in Westminster-Hall*. London, 1746.

Williams, Kelsey Jackson. "Archibald Pitcairne's Liturgical Year." *Studies in Scottish Literature*, vol. 45, no. 2 (2019): 7–14.

Womack, Peter. *Improvement and Romance: Constructing the Myth of the Highlands*. Basingstoke: Macmillan, 1988.

Young Juba: Being the History of the Young Chevalier. London, 1748.

Acknowledgments

The research for this Element was made possible through generous funding by the Social Sciences and Humanities Research Council of Canada. Funding for Open Access was provided by the Department of English, Simon Fraser University. I'd like to thank the many colleagues and students who have provided information, suggestions, questions, and inspiration throughout the writing of this work. Any errors are entirely my fault. To my husband, Rob McGregor, and to my children, Ciaran, Devin and Nia, you are my world, and you make everything possible. Finally, I would like to remember two very close friends who passed on during the writing of this Element: Bud Kurz, musician extraordinaire, and Larrie Cook, who loved books and people. Your memory will live on.

www.ingramcontent.com/pod-product-compliance
Ingram Content Group UK Ltd.
Pitfield, Milton Keynes, MK11 3LW, UK
UKHW030737130225
454942UK00026B/617